Blue Ribbon Baking
from a
Redneck Kitchen

Blue Ribbon Baking
from a
Redneck Kitchen

Francine Bryson

FOREWORD BY **Jeff Foxworthy**

CLARKSON POTTER/PUBLISHERS
NEW YORK

Published in the United States by Clarkson Potter/Publishers,
an imprint of the Crown Publishing Group,
a division of Random House LLC,
a Penguin Random House Company, New York.
www.crownpublishing.com
www.clarksonpotter.com

CLARKSON POTTER is a trademark
and POTTER with colophon is a registered trademark
of Random House LLC.

Library of Congress Cataloging-in-Publication Data
Bryson, Francine.
Blue ribbon baking from a redneck kitchen / Francine Bryson ;
foreword by Jeff Foxworthy ; photographs by Ben Fink. — First edition.
Includes index.
1. Cooking, American—Southern style.
2. Desserts. 3. Baking. I. Title.
TX715.2.S68B795 2014
641.5975—dc23   2014018086

ISBN 978-0-8041-8578-3
eBook ISBN 978-0-8041-8579-0

Printed in the United States of America

Book and cover design by Ashley Tucker
Book and cover photography by Ben Fink

10 9 8 7 6 5 4 3 2 1

First Edition

To Mama, Daddy, Great-Granny,
Granny, and Nana, who taught me
to be the proud Southern woman I am

CONTENTS

Foreword

I remember my first day on the set of the *American Baking Competition*. I had read the profiles of the ten contestants who came from all over the country, half men and half women. There were moms, dads, teachers, and a fireman. Some were loud and others quiet. Their common thread was they all shared a love of baking.

Having watched the British version of the show I knew that the different personalities of the bakers was what made the show so entertaining—and the woman at the station in the back right corner of the room had a barrel full of personality!

I liked Francine from the moment I met her. She was outgoing and funny, and you never had to ask if she was in a good mood or a bad mood. Plus you could tell she knew what she was doing in the kitchen. I quickly learned to hang around her station because she loved to talk and would share a beater covered in icing or a spoonful of something delicious as she created masterpieces.

During pie week each baker had to make a pie from their own recipe. Francine announced to the judges that she was making a chocolate, peanut butter, and bacon pie. I think our British judge, Paul Hollywood, threw up in his mouth just a little bit when he heard that. He said, "That sounds disgusting!" I laughed and said, "I wouldn't bet against her!"

I think my favorite moment on the show came when the judges had to taste the finished pies. Paul took a bite of Francine's, chewed slowly, hung his head for a minute, then looked up, and said, "That is absolutely delicious!" And it was!

I knew at that moment that Francine would go deep in the competition. Week after week, challenge after challenge, she came through. She was full of imagination and came up with recipes that just made you shake your head and laugh until you tried them. Then you were just smiling.

For Francine, cooking is a love language. She talks about learning to make this or that because someone in her family loved it. I remember one day she was making something from her Mama's recipe. As I dipped my finger into the bowl I said, "Tell me about your Mama." Suddenly she stopped stirring and as I looked up I saw her eyes were full of tears. I can only imagine how proud her Mama would be to see her little girl on television in a national baking competition.

As the week of the finals arrived there were only three bakers remaining. On the line was $250,000, a contract for a cookbook, and the title of "America's Best Amateur Baker." One of the finalists really wanted the money to help start her own business. Another finalist wanted the title. When I asked Francine what she wanted the most, she whispered, "The cookbook." See, she has an album full of family recipes that go back to before the turn of the last century, most in their original handwriting. This was a treasure to her, and to share it was her heart's desire.

The pressure during the finale was so thick you could feel it as you entered the room. At one point I walked over to Francine and said, "Don't worry, even if you don't win this competition you are going to have a cookbook. You are too good not to. And I would be honored to write the foreword for you when you do." I am not sure she believed me.

As it turned out the title went to another contestant in a very tight vote. We all hugged, cried a little, and thanked God for the chance to be a part of something like this. It had ended up being one of my favorite projects ever.

Months later, I received an email from Francine saying that she had indeed been given a contract to write a cookbook and she wondered if I was still willing to write a foreword. Are you kidding me? Of course!

So I may not be the sharpest knife in the drawer but it turns out that sometimes I do know what I am talking about. I am excited to finally get to hold this book and to try some of the wonderful recipes compiled here. I am also excited because Francine told me if I was ever near her house that all I had to do was show up and she would cook for me. If you behave, I might even take you with me. It will be worth the trip. I promise.

Bone Appateet!
—Jeff Foxworthy

INTRODUCTION

My life in the kitchen started almost from when I was born. When other young'ins were playing in the yard, I was inside messing with the pots and pans most of the time. I grew up in Greenville, South Carolina, a block away from each of my grandmas—Granny a block up and Nana one down. Me and Mama were always at one house or the other, baking, snacking, chatting. I just loved watching them cook. By the time I got old enough for an Easy Bake oven, we all knew that little light bulb just wasn't going to thrill me. Instead I made my first pie at the age of four. Now I'm not saying it was the *best* pie, but it was a real good starting point, and it shaped my whole life, right there.

Every day after school I was at either Nana or Granny's house and we would cook supper and bake. This is where I formed my love and passion for baking, hearing their stories of cooking through the Depression and how to keep the lights on and feed the kids on a mill worker's pay. I think I realized even then how strong the women were in my family and not to take what we had for granted (it's not like we were rich, but at least we weren't rationing sugar); everything seemed pretty easy compared to those hard days past. Those afternoons formed me into who I am today.

Then, when I was eleven, Daddy and Mama moved our family down to the state of Florida. Leaving my grandmas and the comfort of the hills I was raised in sure wasn't easy. I still baked, but it just wasn't the same without Nana and Granny—and the fruit from those mountain orchards. I spent less time in the kitchen and, with my parents both working, a lot more time doing the household chores instead. I always looked forward to visits back home, or to my grandparents' visits down to see us, because I knew that we would bake together again. I even played hooky from school to spend the day with them in the kitchen, but those ladies could tell I had not really been practicing. Nana even told me that a woman only has so many instincts; it's what you do with them—how much you develop them—that counts.

After my Nana passed when I was fourteen, I sort of lost the thrill of baking for a spell; it just didn't feel right without her. The year I turned sixteen, Daddy came up with the idea that I should enter a food competition, a pork cook-off for the Youth Swine Show in Wakulla, Florida. He must have sensed I needed to get back in the kitchen, that I was missing it. I made an apricot-stuffed pork loin—and it won first place. After that, I was hooked. I found I had a passion for competitive food and I started entering hometown fairs and other contests, all the time honing my skills, learning new tricks and combinations, winning and losing.

I gave up the competition life to run my own household—raise my daughter and be a wife to my husband. But soon I got the itch again and there I was, baking up a storm just like before. I even passed along the gene to Sarablake. When she was a teenager she got real into food competitions and it became our girl time together, just as it had been for me with Mama and my grandmas.

In 2007, Mama passed away suddenly and I came back to South Carolina to take care of Daddy full time. After moving back to my native mountains and doing food competitions in the state and also in North Carolina and parts of Georgia, I found out about the American Pie Council and their pie competition—but I wondered if I was good enough to compete on a national level. The first year I entered and . . . nothing. That was a big ol' get-back-in-the-kitchen-and-practice wake-up call. One woman even warned me not to go back because they said I'd never be that good. Well let me tell you one thing: telling a redneck she can't do something is like waving a red cape in front of a bull. Now I was more determined than ever!

So after a year of trial and error, flopped pies, and bad combinations, I hit on a few ideas that I just knew were amazing. And I guess I wasn't the only one, because my second try at the national competition, not only did I win, but I won for three different pies! I have to say that even better than those ribbons was the new baking family I gained, an amazing group of women and men who have a passion for the art of pie.

After my third year as a member of this prestigious group, Linda Hoskins, the director of the American Pie Council, let us all know about a baking show being cast for CBS. First off, I never would have given a second thought to a television show. But there I was, cooking pork chops for supper on a Thursday night, when I got a call from the casting company asking me to come to Nashville to try out. Well, I thought it was all a big joke, so I hung up and went back to cooking. But my husband, Mark, he went to the computer, looked up the company, and said it was legit. So the next thing I know, I'm off to Nashville, thinking if the whole thing is a flop at least I can see the Ryman Auditorium and the Grand Ole Opry, which were both on my bucket list.

A month later I got another call, this time, "Can you fly to L.A.?," and they mean the *real* one, not lower Alabama. I went and baked and met with people and got to see the Hollywood sign and everything. And when I got home, I got "the call"; I had been cast in *The American Baking Competition,* which sure changed my little ol' life right then and there. Out of the blue, I was baking on TV, meeting people like Paul Hollywood, one of the world's best bakers, and my number-one redneck buddy, Mr. Jeff Foxworthy, who's just the funniest, nicest, most genuine person you could ever meet. I made baking friends I know I'll have forever, and, most important, I got to fulfill my biggest bucket list item ever—my lifelong dream of writing my own cookbook. You see, I collect cookbooks—I've got over 3,000—and read them just like some people tear through romance novels.

For me, the book you're holding in your hands is just the icing on the cake, the biggest, bluest, best ribbon of all.

Here are the recipes and tricks I was taught by my Great-Granny, Granny, Nana, and Mama—the women who schooled me on the ways a Southern woman keeps a kitchen—and that I learned from twenty-plus years of competing on the baking circuit. Now you too can bake up award-winning pies such as Upside-Down Apple-Pecan Pie, fluffy Biscuits Like Nana Made, and irresistible treats like Soda Pop Cake and Classic Southern Lemon Bars—all so good they have made the rounds with the ladies at church, the bridge clubs, supper clubs, and mom groups for generations.

I hope you enjoy baking these recipes as much as I do and share them in your home for years to come with your young'ins, grandbabies, and even great-grandbabies.

Happy baking, y'all!

chapter
1

PIES

Granny's Easy
Butter Crust

Nana's Lard Crust

Buttermilk Crust

Chocolate Crust

Cinnamon Roll Crust

No-Fail, Press-in-Pan Crust

Graham Cracker Crust

Purdy's Peppermint Pie

Pretzel Crust

Chocolate-Key Lime
Heaven Pie

Coconut Cream Pie

I Dream of Bobby Deen
Peanut Butter Pie

Chocolate Silk Pie

White Chocolate-Banana
Cream Pie

Black Tie Strawberry Pie

White Chocolate
Raisin-Nut Pie

Mother-in-Law Pie

Classic Key Lime Pie

Good Ol' Raisin-Oatmeal Pie

Pretzel Pie

Magic Custard Pie

Nana's Apple Pie

Peaches and Cream Pie

Blackberry Blow-Ya-Away
Pie

Winter Fruit Pie

SaraBlake's "Punkin" Pie

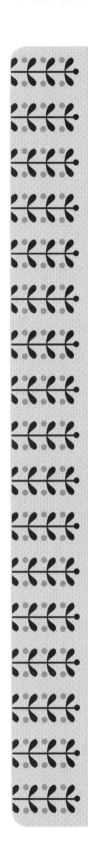

FRANNIE'S·TIPS FOR
Perfect Pie Crust

Over the years, I've sure learned a lot about pies. Lucky for y'all, I'm sharing my wisdom. These pointers will get you on your way to making championship pie crusts:

- **Always** keep your ingredients as ice cold as you can.

- **When you're working with dough,** do not use the palms of your hands—this is where the heat comes from.

- **If the dough starts to get too warm and mushy,** put it in the fridge for a few minutes and it'll harden right up.

- **When you're cutting the fat into the flour,** you can use whatever you have handy—a food processor, pastry cutter, or two knives will all work great. Aim for pea-sized pieces of fat, no smaller.

- **Don't overwork the dough.** This one took me a while to learn, but the more you work those ingredients together, the tougher your pie crust will be.

- **If all else fails,** go for a recipe with a press-in-pan cookie crust. Those are a lot harder to screw up.

Pie crust is easier than you think. Just keep it simple, don't be too hard on yourself, and never think, "If it ain't perfect, it ain't worth it." That's just not how it works. You'll get there—just keep trying!

Granny's easy Butter Crust

No matter who's asking, I tell them that this is my simple, works-every-time dough. Granny (my dad's mom) taught it to me way back when, and I've been using it ever since. For anyone who doesn't like using Crisco or lard, meet your new favorite pie dough.

This one's a go-to for Thanksgiving, when I'm running around the kitchen like a chicken with its head cut off. Make a big batch of this dough in advance, throw it in the freezer, then thaw it and roll it when you need it. Then you can fill your pies up with pecan, apple, or sweet potato filling—or whatever you like after that big old turkey.

INGREDIENTS

1 cup all-purpose flour, plus more for rolling

3 tablespoons sugar

Pinch of salt

½ cup (1 stick) unsalted butter, cut into pieces, cold

1 teaspoon pure vanilla extract (optional)

DIRECTIONS

Whisk together the flour, sugar, and salt until fully mixed. Then, using a pastry cutter, two knives, or a food processor, cut in the butter until it forms pea-sized clumps. If using, stir in the vanilla extract. You can roll this dough straightaway; there is no need to chill it first.

To bake the crust, see page 21.

Makes one 9- or 10-inch pie crust

 BLUE RIBBON TIP Although it's listed here as optional, I love throwing in a little bit of vanilla extract—it enhances all the flavors going on in the pie.

Nana's Lard Crust

Down South, we aren't afraid of baking with lard; in fact, we believe in it on principle. This recipe makes just the flakiest crust you could ever imagine. Nana (my mom's mom) taught me how to make it when I was four, round about when I baked my first pie! From then on, I was rolling out pie dough, standing on a chair to reach the counter. In my family, the cornerstone of baking was (and still is) knowing how to make your own pie dough and biscuits.

I've found lard in most grocery stores today; they sell it in buckets or 1-pound blocks in the baking aisle. If you can't find lard, or don't love it as much as my Nana did, you can substitute Crisco shortening (either regular or the butter-flavored baking version).

INGREDIENTS

2½ cups all-purpose flour

Pinch of salt

¾ cup lard

6 to 7 tablespoons cold water, as needed

DIRECTIONS

Put the flour and salt in a bowl, add the lard, and crumble the lard until you have pea-sized clumps. Add the cold water, 1 tablespoon at a time, until the dough just sticks together. Roll into a ball, cover with plastic wrap, and refrigerate for 20 minutes before using, or freeze for up to 3 months and defrost before rolling. To bake the crust, see opposite.

MAKES ONE 9- OR 10-INCH PIE CRUST

 BLUE RIBBON TIP This dough works real well with extra-juicy fruit pies, and I use it for apple, blackberry, and peach pies.

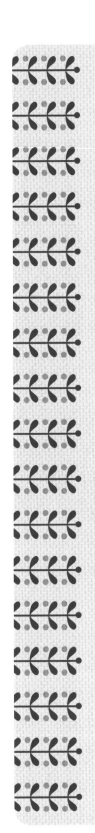

BLIND BaKING
A PIE CRUST

To fully bake a crust—including any one of these: Granny's Easy Butter Crust (page 19), Nana's Lard Crust (page 20), Buttermilk Crust (page 22), Chocolate Crust (page 23), and Cinnamon Roll Crust (page 24)—follow the directions below. Filling the crust with weights helps it keep its shape.

- Preheat the oven to 350°F.

- Dust your counter with flour or top it with a sheet of wax paper. Roll the chilled dough until it is 1 inch larger than your pie pan. Prick the dough with a fork.

- Roll the dough up onto your pin and unroll it over your pie pan. Settle it into your pan. Make a decorative edge if you'd like by pinching the dough between your thumbs and forefingers or crimping it with a pastry crimper or fork. Remove any excess dough.

- Put a large square of aluminum foil over the pie pan and gently press it into the crust. Fill the crust with ceramic pie weights or dried beans.

- Bake the crust for 20 to 25 minutes. Carefully remove the foil and weights and bake until evenly light brown, an additional 8 to 11 minutes.

- Let cool completely before filling.

BUTTERMILK CRUST

This was Mama's recipe. She didn't have too many from-scratch recipes, but this was one she did real well. This pie dough works with many different fillings, and the buttermilk gives it a nice tang, balancing sweet fillings. Combining two fats—shortening and butter—makes the dough flexible and easy to work with. This makes two crusts; I usually bake one and keep the dough for a second one in the freezer until I need it.

INGREDIENTS

2½ cups all-purpose flour

2 tablespoons sugar

1 teaspoon salt

½ cup (1 stick) unsalted butter, cut into pieces, cold

½ cup shortening (I use Crisco), cut into pieces, cold

¼ cup well-shaken buttermilk

DIRECTIONS

Combine the flour, sugar, and salt in a large bowl. Using a pastry cutter, two knives, or a food processor, cut in the butter and shortening until they form pea-sized clumps. Add the buttermilk and stir with a fork until bigger clumps form. Press together to form a dough and then divide the dough in half. Form two balls of dough, wrap separately in plastic wrap, and refrigerate for 1 hour before using, or freeze for up to 3 months and defrost before using.

To bake the crust, see page 21.

MAKES TWO 9- OR 10-INCH PIE CRUSTS, OR ENOUGH DOUGH FOR 1 DOUBLE-CRUST PIE

 BLUE RIBBON TIP If you can't find buttermilk, or don't feel like buying a whole gallon of it (I only buy it when I'm making big batches of biscuits), put 1 teaspoon white vinegar or lemon juice into 1 cup milk, shake it in a mason jar or stir it with a spoon, and let it sit for a few minutes.

CHOCOLATE CRUST

This recipe's an old one—it's been around for what feels like forever. I use it for any type of pie or tart—my favorite's a cream-peach tart (you wouldn't think they go together, peaches and chocolate, but just give it a try!). Even though it's chocolate, it's not too sweet.

The ingredients are a little different than for your basic crust—the egg yolk binds everything together and the confectioner's sugar gives a great texture. I like to use espresso powder in this crust, too, because it gives a hint of that coffee-chocolate flavor and keeps the crust from getting oversweet.

INGREDIENTS

- 1¼ cups all-purpose flour
- ¼ cup unsweetened cocoa powder
- ½ teaspoon espresso powder (optional)
- ½ cup (1 stick) unsalted butter, at room temperature
- ½ cup confectioner's sugar
- 1 large egg yolk
- 1 teaspoon vanilla butter and nut flavoring (see Blue Ribbon Tip, below)

DIRECTIONS

In a bowl, sift together the flour, cocoa, and espresso powder, if using.

In a separate bowl, mix together the butter and sugar until smooth and creamy. Mix in the egg yolk and vanilla butter and nut flavoring until smooth. Slowly add the dry ingredients and mix until just combined.

Roll into a ball, wrap with plastic wrap, and refrigerate for 1 hour before using, or freeze for up to 3 months and defrost before rolling.

To bake the crust, see page 21.

MAKES ONE 9- OR 10-INCH PIE CRUST OR TART CRUST

 BLUE RIBBON TIP Around here, I get vanilla butter and nut flavoring locally, but I know McCormick makes one that should be available at most grocers. If you can't find it, ask your grocer to order some, or just use half vanilla extract and half almond extract.

CINNaMON ROLL CRUST

I got this recipe from a friend of mine—it's quick, easy, and it looks real cool. If you're scared to make a homemade crust, this is a great way to get your feet wet, and if you're short on time, or just want a change from plain old crust, try this out.

The cinnamon in the dough is nice with pumpkin, sweet potato, or apple filling—perfect for fall. To make sure none of the filling slips through, be sure to mash up the crust real good and close up any holes and gaps. If you're baking with kids, this is a recipe that's hard to mess up.

INGREDIENTS

- 2 (9-inch) store-bought refrigerated pie crusts (I use Pillsbury, which has 2 crusts in a package)

- 2 tablespoons plus 2 teaspoons ($\frac{1}{3}$ stick) unsalted butter, melted

- $\frac{1}{4}$ cup ground cinnamon (enough to fully cover the dough)
- 3 tablespoons firmly packed light brown sugar

DIRECTIONS

Remove the pie crusts from the refrigerator and let sit in the package for 20 minutes at room temperature.

Unroll both pie crusts from the package and brush with the butter. If you don't have a pastry brush, use a spoon to drizzle the butter over the crusts. Mix together the cinnamon and brown sugar and then sprinkle evenly over both crusts. Tightly roll each crust to make two logs, and then slice each one into $\frac{1}{4}$-inch-thick circles.

Press the slices into a 9- or 10-inch pie pan, starting from the middle and working your way out to the rim. Using your fingers, mash the slices together so there are no gaps or holes, and the crust is entirely solid.

To bake the crust, see page 21.

MAKES ONE 9- OR 10-INCH PIE CRUST

NO-Fail, Press-IN-PaN Crust

After I'd made some failed first attempts at rolling out pie dough, my Granny taught me the ways of the press-in-pan crust. This one is hard to mess up, but don't go trying. You can use this crust with any kind of pie, and it won't give you any trouble.

INGREDIENTS

1½ cups all-purpose flour

2 teaspoons sugar

Pinch of salt

2 tablespoons whole milk

½ cup vegetable oil

DIRECTIONS

Preheat the oven to 350°F.

Stir together the flour, sugar, and salt in a bowl until fully combined. While stirring, add the milk and then slowly pour in the oil. Mix well with a fork (this will help to get rid of clumps), then dump into a 9- or 10-inch pie pan, and use your fingertips to pat out to fit the pan. Make sure to press the mixture evenly into the pan so it will cook evenly.

Bake until nice and browned, about 9 minutes. Let cool completely before filling.

Makes One 9- Or 10-INCH Pie Crust

GRAHAM CRACKER CRUST

This crust is a simple one, and absolutely anyone can make it. It's perfect for cream pies (a cream pie ain't a cream pie without a cookie crust, in my opinion), especially banana; coconut; my favorite, Key lime; and even lemon meringue. To crush the crackers, I usually put them in a plastic bag and go to town with a rolling pin, but feel free to use a food processor, if you like.

INGREDIENTS ....

1 cup graham cracker crumbs (about 14 crackers)

⅓ cup sugar

¼ cup (4 tablespoons) unsalted butter, melted

DIRECTIONS ....

Preheat the oven to 350°F.

Mix together the graham cracker crumbs, sugar, and butter. I usually use a spatula because it crushes the crumbs even more, but use anything you like—a spoon, your hands, or a whisk. Firmly and evenly press the mixture onto the bottom and up the sides of a 9-inch pie pan.

Bake until deep golden brown, 8 to 10 minutes. Let cool completely before filling.

MAKES ONE 9-INCH PIE CRUST

 BLUE RIBBON TIP A good trick to remember is to watch the graham crackers after you mix in the butter. They'll go from tan to dark brown when they're fully coated with butter and ready to bake.

more cookie crusts

If you can crumble a cookie, you can make a pie crust out of it, so get to crushing, y'all! My go-to is Milano cookies (especially with raspberry filling, oh my . . .). Use the baking instructions opposite with these combos:

- **pepperidge farm milano cookie crust** Crush the entire 6-ounce bag with 2½ tablespoons melted unsalted butter for a 9-inch crust.

- **oreo cookie crust** Use 25 crushed Oreos with 3 tablespoons melted unsalted butter for a 9-inch crust.

- **chocolate chip cookie crust** Use 25 crushed Chips Ahoy! cookies with 3 tablespoons melted unsalted butter for a 9-inch crust.

PURDY'S PEPPERMINT PIE

If you're looking to make a holiday pie, this is the one. In my house, it ain't Christmas without it! Around here, we love those soft peppermints (I buy Bobs, which you can find online), and that's how this pie came about. The chocolate crust and the peppermint filling go together real nice, especially with a cup of hot cocoa.

If you're wondering who Purdy is, that's me—my husband calls me "Purdy," and whenever I'm making a pie, he says to me, "Make sure it's purdy, Purdy."

INGREDIENTS

1 envelope unflavored powdered gelatin

2¼ cups cold water

2 cups heavy cream

1 (8-ounce) bag soft peppermints (see Blue Ribbon Tip, below)

1 fully baked 9-inch Chocolate Crust (page 23)

10 starlight peppermints, crushed

DIRECTIONS

Stir the gelatin into the water and set aside at room temperature.

In a saucepan, combine ½ cup of the heavy cream and the peppermints over low heat, stirring occasionally, until all of the peppermints have melted.

Stir the gelatin mixture into the peppermint mixture until combined. Transfer to a bowl and let cool.

Whip the remaining 1½ cups cream until stiff. Fold the whipped cream into the cooled peppermint mixture and pour into the pie crust. Top with the crushed peppermints. Refrigerate until serving, at least 2 hours and up to 2 days.

MAKES ONE 9-INCH PIE

 BLUE RIBBON TIPS You must use *soft* peppermints here; hard ones will take at least twice as long to melt and just aren't the same.

If you are feeling fancy, melt some white chocolate and drizzle it over the pie before topping with the starlight mints.

pretzel crust

Like many of my recipes, this one came about from just messing around in the kitchen, looking for something different. This crust is perfect if you're looking for some salty with the sweet. Try it with a real sweet filling, like caramel cream, chocolate, or butterscotch—the pretzels will balance out all the sugar. Like with graham crackers, you can crush the pretzels with a plastic bag and a rolling pin— or in a food processor. I find skinny pretzel sticks the easiest to crush.

INGREDIENTS

- ¾ cup (1½ sticks) unsalted butter, melted, plus more for the pan
- 2 cups finely crushed pretzels
- ¼ cup firmly packed light brown sugar
- ½ teaspoon pure vanilla extract

DIRECTIONS

Preheat the oven to 350°F. Lightly grease a 9-inch pie pan.

Stir together the pretzels, butter, brown sugar, and vanilla until fully combined. Firmly and evenly press the mixture onto the bottom and up the sides of the prepared pie pan.

Bake until lightly browned, 10 to 12 minutes. Let cool completely before filling.

MAKES ONE 9-INCH PIE CRUST

CHOCOLATE-KEY LIME HEAVEN PIE

This pie won third place in the amateur citrus division at the 2013 APC Crisco National Pie Championships, and it's one of my favorite pies out there. I came up with this one after tasting something at the competition the year before—there was a long line of folks waiting at a booth, hooting and hollering. Turns out they were going crazy for chocolate-dipped frozen Key lime pie on a stick, and the minute I tried it, I just knew I had to make a pie out of it. People don't think about dark chocolate with Key lime, but the bitter chocolate balances out the cool, sweet citrus. If you've got Key limes, all the better, but this still tastes great with just plain old limes, too. Top with sweetened whipped cream, if you'd like.

INGREDIENTS

- 1 (11-ounce) package white chocolate chips
- 1 cup plus 3 tablespoons heavy cream
- 1 tablespoon sour cream
- 1 teaspoon grated lime zest
- ⅓ cup fresh lime juice
- 1 fully baked Oreo Cookie Crust (page 27)
- 4 ounces bittersweet chocolate, chopped

DIRECTIONS

In a small saucepan over medium heat, melt together the white chocolate chips with 1 cup of the heavy cream until smooth. Remove from the heat and stir in the sour cream, lime zest, and lime juice. Pour into the cooled crust and refrigerate for 30 minutes.

In a microwave or double boiler, melt the bittersweet chocolate and remaining 3 tablespoons heavy cream; stir until smooth. Let cool to room temperature, about 15 minutes.

Pour the bittersweet chocolate over the pie and refrigerate for at least 2 hours or overnight.

MAKES ONE 9-INCH PIE

COCONUT CREAM PIE

Around these parts, coconut cream pie's a staple, especially in the spring when there's that first hint of summer weather. That's when I start dragging out all the chilled cream pies—Key lime, banana cream—all those real fancy-looking ones.

This recipe is in honor of my Mama—it was her quick go-to pie for company, and everyone just always went nuts for it. She'd throw it in the refrigerator early in the day, then after supper, out it came, cool and creamy and real impressive looking. I've changed the recipe around some over the years and switched up the filling, but the crust is all Mama in the kitchen.

This pie's got a real strong coconut flavor, on account of using shredded coconut and ice-cold coconut cream in the crust. For the pudding, make sure to use the powder mix, not premade, and if you're having a hard time finding the cream of coconut, look near the liquor mixers, it's usually in that aisle.

INGREDIENTS ....

crust
- ½ cup sweetened shredded coconut
- 1¼ cups all-purpose flour, plus more for rolling
- Pinch of salt
- ½ cup (1 stick) unsalted butter, cut in pieces, cold
- 3 to 5 tablespoons cream of coconut, cold, as needed

filling
- 1 cup unsweetened shredded coconut
- 1 (5.1-ounce) box French vanilla instant pudding mix
- 1 (15-ounce) can cream of coconut
- ½ cup whole milk
- 2 cups heavy cream
- 1 teaspoon pure vanilla extract
- 3 tablespoons sugar
- 1½ (8-ounce) packages cream cheese, at room temperature

DIRECTIONS ....

Make the crust: Pulse the sweetened shredded coconut in a food processor until finely chopped. Add the flour and salt and pulse again to mix.

Add the butter to the flour mixture and pulse until the butter pieces are pea-sized. One tablespoon at a time, pulse in the coconut cream as needed, until the dough just comes together. Turn the dough out onto a piece of plastic wrap and form into a disk. Wrap and refrigerate for at least 20 minutes and up to 1 hour.

Preheat the oven to 375°F.

Roll the dough on a floured work surface until it is 1 inch larger than your pie pan. Gently press it into a 9-inch pie pan and crimp the edges with a fork or a pastry crimper. Set a large piece of foil over the pie pan and gently press it into the crust. Fill the crust with ceramic pie weights or dried beans and bake the crust for 15 minutes. Carefully remove the foil and weights and bake until the bottom is cooked through, an additional 10 minutes. Let cool completely before filling.

Meanwhile, reduce the oven temperature to 350°F.

Start the filling: Spread the unsweetened shredded coconut onto a baking sheet and toast in the oven, stirring once, until just golden, 3 to 5 minutes. Set aside to cool.

Combine the pudding mix, cream of coconut, and milk in a large glass jar or bowl. Cover the jar tightly and shake for 1 to 2 minutes, or mix with a whisk until well combined. Refrigerate until ready to use.

Using an electric mixer, whip the heavy cream, vanilla extract, and sugar until fluffy, then cover and refrigerate.

In a separate bowl, beat the cream cheese until smooth. Gradually beat the pudding mixture into the cream cheese, scraping the bowl regularly to eliminate clumps. Fold in half of the whipped cream with a rubber spatula. Carefully mix until smooth and then scoop into the cooled crust. Top with the remaining whipped cream and sprinkle generously with the toasted coconut. Refrigerate overnight before serving.

MAKES ONE 9-INCH PIE

I DREAM OF BOBBY DEEN PEANUT BUTTER PIE

Recipes come from the darnedest places, and I ain't joking: This pie come to me in a dream. I was in an all-red kitchen—red countertops, red backsplash, red tile floor, and red appliances—with Mr. Bobby Deen. He's a looker, that one. Anyhow, we were cooking up some pie in this dream, and—would you believe it—the recipe really works! It's one of the best things I ever made, and it came to me in a dream, of all things.

The creamy peanut butter filling's got a mousse-like texture, light and airy. The crust is all coconut—no rolling pins for this one—just mash it all together and the natural coconut sugars make the crust! This is a real hometown pie; I make it for the family and to bring to friends (of course, I'm the one who has to bring dessert).

INGREDIENTS

crust

2½ cups sweetened shredded coconut

4 tablespoons (½ stick) unsalted butter, melted

¼ cup heavy cream

1 cup semisweet chocolate chips

filling

2 cups heavy cream

¾ cup confectioner's sugar

1 (8-ounce) package cream cheese, at room temperature

½ cup granulated sugar

½ cup creamy peanut butter (I use Jif)

DIRECTIONS

Preheat the oven to 350°F.

Make the crust: Put the coconut on a baking sheet and toast, stirring a few times, until evenly browned, 10 to 16 minutes. Let cool.

Mix the toasted coconut with the butter and evenly press into a 10-inch deep-dish pie pan. Put in the refrigerator to set, 20 minutes.

Heat the cream in a saucepan until warm, but not scalding. Remove from the heat, add the chocolate chips, and stir until melted. Spread the chocolate over the chilled coconut crust and refrigerate until set, about 15 minutes.

Make the filling: Using an electric mixer, whip the heavy cream and confectioner's sugar until the cream holds stiff peaks. Do not overwhip. Scoop up 1 cup of the whipped cream, put it in a bowl in the refrigerator, and reserve for garnishing the pie.

In a separate bowl, using an electric mixer, whip the cream cheese and granulated sugar on medium speed until fluffy, then add the peanut butter and mix until fully blended. Gently fold the remaining whipped cream into the cream cheese mixture with a rubber spatula. Pour the mixture into the pie crust and chill in the refrigerator, at least 1 hour or overnight.

Top with the reserved 1 cup whipped cream.

MAKES ONE 10-INCH DEEP-DISH PIE

 BLUE RIBBON TIP When you press out the crust, make sure it's completely even the whole way around. If you don't, there'll be soft spots, which don't make for a dream-worthy pie!

CHOCOLATE SILK PIE

This pie is my Daddy's absolute favorite, and Great-Grandma always used to make it special for him whenever family got together. My Granny called this one "Depression Pie" because she remembers baking it way back then, when all your food got bought with ration tickets and chocolate and sugar were luxury items. People from that time seemed to stay in that mode, always scrimping and saving—when my Great-Grandma passed, we went through her house and found a 150-pound bag of sugar, just in case.

Now this pie is a fourth-generation dessert, and I make it for my daughter, too. I adapted it because the old method was too dang time-consuming, but the recipe still uses raw eggs; there weren't salmonella scares back then when everyone just got eggs from their chickens out back. I make it the same way, with eggs from my chickens, and it makes for a real rich, silky filling.

INGREDIENTS

- 8 ounces bittersweet or semisweet chocolate
- ¼ teaspoon espresso powder
- 1½ cups heavy cream
- 1 cup (2 sticks) salted butter, at room temperature
- 1½ cups sugar
- 1 teaspoon pure vanilla extract
- 4 large eggs, at room temperature
- 1 fully baked 9-inch pie crust (I like to use Granny's Easy Butter Crust, page 19)

DIRECTIONS

Microwave half of the chocolate in 20-second intervals, stirring in between, until completely melted. Stir in the espresso powder. Set aside and let cool to room temperature, 10 to 15 minutes.

Whip the cream until it holds stiff peaks.

Using the paddle attachment of an electric stand mixer (or a hand mixer), beat together the butter and sugar until fluffy. Add the cooled melted chocolate and beat on medium-low speed until combined. Mix in the vanilla.

Switch to the whisk attachment (or continue with a hand mixer), add 1 of the eggs, and whip for 5 minutes on medium speed. Repeat with the remaining 3 eggs, beating for an additional 2 minutes after adding each one. Fold in half of the whipped cream using a rubber spatula.

Pour the filling into the baked pie crust, top with the remaining whipped cream, and refrigerate for 3 hours.

Using a vegetable peeler, shave the remaining chocolate into thin pieces and sprinkle over the pie before serving.

MAKES ONE 9-INCH PIE

 BLUE RIBBON TIP I like using salted butter here because it goes so great with the chocolate and means I don't have to measure out a separate ingredient.

WHITE CHOCOLATE-BANANA CREAM PIE

It doesn't happen often, but sometimes you can fight about pie. One day, when I was about ten or eleven years old, me and Mama got in an argument: I wanted to make coconut cream pie and she was in the mood for banana cream. We decided to compromise, and after messing around with some ripe bananas, this is what we came up with. I added the white chocolate because I just love it so much.

Homemade pudding is a lost art these days, but a real banana cream pie's just gotta have it. I like to use an unbaked graham cracker crust here because it's nice and soft. I usually top the pie with more white chocolate (ain't no surprise there), but you can use regular chocolate or a few extra banana slices instead.

INGREDIENTS

crust

- 2 cups graham cracker crumbs (about 28 crackers)
- ½ cup (1 stick) unsalted butter, melted
- ½ cup sugar

white chocolate layer

- 6 ounces white chocolate baking squares (I use Baker's)
- 2 tablespoons unsalted butter
- ⅓ cup half-and-half

filling

- 1½ cups half-and-half
- ¾ cup sugar
- 3 tablespoons cornstarch
- 3 large egg yolks
- 1 teaspoon pure vanilla extract
- 1 tablespoon unsalted butter

- 3 to 4 bananas, as needed, sliced
- 8 ounces frozen nondairy whipped topping, thawed
- White chocolate curls

Make the crust: In a bowl, stir together the graham cracker crumbs, butter, and sugar until the mixture becomes dark brown and the crumbs are fully coated. Press onto the bottom and up the sides of a 9-inch deep-dish pie pan. Refrigerate until cool, at least 15 minutes.

Make the white chocolate layer: In a saucepan, melt the white chocolate and butter with the half-and-half over low heat. Stir until smooth. Pour the mixture into the cooled crust and refrigerate for 30 minutes.

While the crust is cooling, prepare the filling: In a bowl, whisk together the half-and-half, sugar, cornstarch, and egg yolks well and then pour into a medium saucepan. Heat over medium-low heat and cook, whisking constantly, until the mixture starts to thicken into a pudding; do not let the eggs curdle. Remove from the heat and stir in the vanilla extract and butter. Pour into a bowl, press a piece of plastic wrap against the surface, and refrigerate until chilled, at least 20 minutes.

Layer the sliced bananas over the white chocolate in the pie crust and then pour the cooled custard over it. Top with the whipped topping and white chocolate curls.

MAKES ONE 9-INCH DEEP-DISH PIE

 BLUE RIBBON TIP If you want to make classic banana cream pie, just leave out the white chocolate, and you've got a solid, simple staple.

Black Tie Strawberry Pie

Some of my best recipes happen by accident, when I'm just playing around in the kitchen and having some fun. I came up with this one when I was trying things out for a competition, and, would you believe, it ended up being the winning dish of the 2012 South Carolina State Strawberry Festival! It's called "black tie pie" on account of the chocolate and cream, and it's the tastiest tuxedo you'll ever try.

There's a bunch of steps to this pie, and it may look a little complicated, but it's worth it. This pie's best when strawberries are in season and nice and sweet. I like to use animal crackers in the crust because they—and a dusting of unsweetened cocoa at the end—balance the sweetness of the other ingredients.

INGREDIENTS

chocolate layer
- 1 (12-ounce) package semisweet chocolate chips
- ½ cup heavy cream

crust
- 1½ cups crushed animal crackers
- ½ cup ground almonds (see Blue Ribbon Tip, opposite)

- 5 tablespoons unsalted butter, melted
- 2 pints strawberries, thinly sliced, plus a few whole berries for garnish

filling
- 1 (8-ounce) package cream cheese, at room temperature
- ½ cup granulated sugar

- ½ cup heavy cream, cold
- 2 large eggs
- 1 teaspoon pure vanilla extract

garnish
- 1 cup heavy cream
- 1½ tablespoons confectioner's sugar
- ½ teaspoon unsweetened cocoa powder

DIRECTIONS

Preheat the oven to 350°F.

Make the chocolate layer: Melt the chocolate chips and heavy cream in a double-boiler or in the microwave, stirring until smooth.

Make the crust: In a separate bowl, combine the crushed cookies, ground almonds, and butter and mix thoroughly. Press into a 10-inch pie pan, fully covering the bottom and sides. Spread half of the chocolate mixture on the bottom and sides of the crust; reserve the rest at room temperature. Fill the crust with the strawberries.

Make the filling: Using an electric mixer, mix the cream cheese and granulated sugar on medium speed until smooth. Pour in the cream and whip until it holds stiff peaks. Add the eggs and vanilla extract and mix until combined.

Pour the cream cheese mixture over the strawberries in the crust and bake until the middle is fully set and a knife inserted into the middle comes out clean, 25 minutes. The strawberries will rise up and bake into the creamy mixture, making a kind of cheesecake. Transfer the pie to the refrigerator to cool for at least 2 hours or overnight.

When ready to serve, top with the remaining chocolate mixture, remelting it if need be. Whip the cream to stiff peaks and spoon it over the chocolate. Stir together the confectioner's sugar and cocoa powder and dust the top of the pie. Garnish with strawberries, if desired.

MAKES ONE 10-INCH PIE

 BLUE RIBBON TIP I grind my almonds for this recipe in a coffee grinder. The texture is coarser than almond flour, which is too fine to use here.

WHITE CHOCOLATE RAISIN-NUT PIE

Trial, error, and a whole lot of hours with my oven brought me this recipe, which ended up winning the blue ribbon at the Crisco baking competition in 2012. This ain't no small competition, but, you know, this ain't no small pie! It's an easy pie to eat, and I guess those judges thought so, too. For the competition, I used the basic Crisco pie crust required by national competition standards, but I also like it with my Granny's or Nana's crust, too.

INGREDIENTS ....

filling
- 1½ cups apple juice
- 2 cups raisins
- 2 (8-ounce) packages Philadelphia Indulgence white chocolate cream cheese spread, at room temperature
- ⅔ cup granulated sugar
- ¼ teaspoon salt

- 2 large eggs
- ⅔ cup heavy cream
- 1 teaspoon pure vanilla extract
- 1 cup chopped toasted pecans

- 1 unbaked 9-inch pie crust

topping
- 1 cup heavy cream
- ⅔ cup confectioner's sugar
- 1¼ teaspoons pure vanilla extract

DIRECTIONS

Preheat the oven to 350°F.

Make the filling: In a saucepan over medium-high heat, combine the apple juice and raisins and simmer until the raisins are plump and rehydrated, about 15 minutes. Drain the raisins, discarding the apple juice, and let cool.

Using an electric mixer, beat the cream cheese spread until smooth. Mix in the granulated sugar, salt, eggs, cream, and vanilla extract. Stir in the raisins and pecans and pour into the pie crust.

Bake until the center is soft but completely set, 35 to 40 minutes. Refrigerate for at least 2 hours or overnight.

Prepare the topping: Whip the cream with the confectioner's sugar and vanilla extract until stiff peaks form. Spread over the chilled pie and serve.

MAKES ONE 9-INCH PIE

 BLUE RIBBON TIP Apple juice (my favorite juice there is) plumps up the raisins, so they're sweet and juicy and not too chewy.

MOTHer-IN-LaW PIe

Any wife knows that if mama-in-law ain't happy, nobody's happy. When birthdays or holidays roll around, my husband's mother doesn't let me buy her anything, so I bake for her—pies, cookies, cakes, whatever she likes. This special pie is my gift to her for Mother's Day because she loves a hint of chocolate that's not too sweet. I know I ought to be modest, but there aren't words for how amazing this pie is: chocolate, cheesecake, cherries, and raspberries. If you're looking to impress, try this one out (especially for your mother-in-law!).

INGREDIENTS

- 1 (12-ounce) package semisweet chocolate chips
- 1⅓ cups heavy cream
- 4 tablespoons (½ stick) unsalted butter, cut into pieces
- 1 fully baked Raspberry Milano Cookie Crust (page 27)
- 1 (15-ounce) can cherry pie filling
- 1 (8-ounce) package cream cheese, at room temperature
- ¾ cup confectioner's sugar
- 1 tablespoon pure vanilla extract
- 2 large eggs

DIRECTIONS

Preheat the oven to 350°F.

Microwave the chocolate chips and ⅔ cup of the cream in a heat-safe bowl in two or three 30-second spurts, stirring between each, until the chocolate begins to melt. Whisk in the butter until smooth. Let cool, stirring occasionally, until the mixture reaches a spreadable consistency, 5 to 10 minutes.

Spoon half of the chocolate mixture into the crust; put the rest of the chocolate mixture aside. Pour the cherry pie filling into the crust.

Using an electric mixer, beat the cream cheese, ½ cup of the confectioner's sugar, the vanilla extract, and eggs on medium speed until smooth. Pour the cream cheese mixture evenly over the cherry pie filling.

Bake until the center is set, about 30 minutes. Remove from the oven and let cool on a wire rack. Cover, and chill in the refrigerator for at least 4 hours or overnight.

Whip the remaining ⅔ cup cream with the remaining ¼ cup confectioner's sugar until it holds stiff peaks. Spoon over the chilled pie and drizzle the remaining chocolate on top; remelt the chocolate in the microwave if needed.

MAKES ONE 9-INCH PIE

CLassic Key Lime Pie

When you bake (and eat) as much pie as I do, you get real good at your favorites, and my ultimate, number-one favorite pie is Key lime. Growing up, my family moved to Florida for a few years and that's where I learned how to make the real thing. My aunt Eva taught me this recipe when I was about thirteen years old and I've been making it ever since. I love the sweet and tartness together, and, of course, the fluffy sticky meringue on top. If you don't already know how, y'all have to learn how to make a real meringue.

INGREDIENTS

1 (14-ounce) can sweetened condensed milk

2 tablespoons grated lemon zest

1 tablespoon grated lime zest

3 tablespoons fresh lime juice, preferably Key lime

4 large egg yolks

1 cup heavy cream, cold

1 unbaked Graham Cracker Crust (page 26)

4 large egg whites

1 teaspoon cream of tartar

6 tablespoons sugar

DIRECTIONS

Preheat the oven to 350°F.

In a large bowl, whisk together the condensed milk, lemon zest, lime zest, lime juice, egg yolks, and cream. Pour into the pie crust. Bake until the filling doesn't jiggle in the middle when the pie is nudged, 25 to 35 minutes. Let cool completely. Keep the oven on.

Using an electric mixer, whip the egg whites with the cream of tartar and sugar until the whites are glossy and firm.

Spread the meringue over the cooled pie and bake for 10 minutes, or until the meringue tips are golden. Refrigerate for about 2 hours before serving.

MaKes One 9-INCH Pie

GOOD OL' RAISIN-OATMEAL PIE

Not every pie needs razzle-dazzle—sometimes you just want a solid, good pie. So when I'm in the mood for something basic, I make one of these. Oatmeal and raisins are a real good old-school combination, and not too sweet. This pie will hold up for a few days, and it's nice to have in the afternoon with a big cup of coffee.

INGREDIENTS

crust
- 1½ cups all-purpose flour
- 1 teaspoon salt
- 1½ teaspoons granulated sugar
- 2 tablespoons whole milk
- ½ cup vegetable oil

filling
- 3 large eggs
- 1 cup light corn syrup
- ½ cup firmly packed light brown sugar
- 3 tablespoons unsalted butter or margarine, melted
- ¾ cup quick-cooking rolled oats
- 1 tablespoon all-purpose flour
- 1 teaspoon ground cinnamon
- ¼ teaspoon salt
- 1½ cups raisins

DIRECTIONS

Prepare the crust: Mix the flour, salt, and granulated sugar in a 9-inch pie pan. Add the milk and oil. Mix well with a fork and press onto the bottom and up the sides of the pie pan.

Preheat the oven to 325°F.

Make the filling: Mix together the eggs, corn syrup, brown sugar, and butter with a whisk. Add the oats, flour, cinnamon, salt, and raisins and mix until fully combined. Pour into the pie crust and set on a baking sheet.

Bake until the top is golden brown, 45 to 50 minutes. Let cool completely on a wire rack before serving.

MAKES ONE 9-INCH PIE

 BLUE RIBBON TIP Make sure to put your pie pan on a baking sheet; otherwise, the pie will bubble over and destroy your oven if you aren't careful!

PRETZEL PIE

When I first saw Christy Jordan, one of our favorite bakers down here, making pretzel pie, I knew I had to come up with my own version. Because, while I love making pecan pie, nuts are so dang expensive! The pretzels in this pie are salty and crunchy, just like nuts, but won't break the bank. People don't realize how good pretzel pie is—cheap *and* delicious. I like it for Thanksgiving. When you're spending a small fortune at the grocery store and hours in the kitchen, saving time and money ain't half bad!

You can use any kind of pretzels; the cheaper, the better. I often use pretzel rods and crush them up real good with a wooden spoon. And while I usually go for homemade crusts, on this pie you've got to use a store-bought one; it's thicker and tougher and it'll absorb all the juices.

INGREDIENTS

filling
- 4 large eggs
- 1 cup granulated sugar
- ½ cup firmly packed light brown sugar
- ¾ cup dark corn syrup
- ½ cup (1 stick) unsalted butter, melted
- 1½ teaspoons pure vanilla extract
- 1 (9-inch) store-bought refrigerated deep-dish pie crust

topping
- 1½ cups crushed pretzels
- 3 tablespoons unsalted butter, melted
- 3 tablespoons granulated sugar
- 1 teaspoon ground cinnamon

DIRECTIONS

Preheat the oven to 350°F.

Make the filling: In a bowl, whisk together the eggs, granulated sugar, brown sugar, corn syrup, butter, and vanilla until well combined. Pour into the pie crust.

Prepare the topping: Stir together the pretzels, butter, granulated sugar, and cinnamon until the pretzels are fully coated. Sprinkle over the pie.

Bake for 30 minutes. Cover the edges with foil to avoid burning and continue to bake until set around the edges and the center jiggles slightly, about 30 minutes more. Let cool completely on a wire rack before serving.

MAKES ONE 9-INCH DEEP-DISH PIE

MAGIC CUSTARD PIE

When a pie's been around this long, you know it's got to be a good one. This one's probably seventy-five years old and there must be a hundred versions or more. It's been called everything in the book—my Nana used to call it "Egg Custard Pie," but I call it "Magic Custard Pie." Why "magic"? Because it makes its own crust—ain't much more magical than that! The flour settles into the pie while it bakes, and you've got yourself a crust; try baking it in a glass pie dish and you can see the crust forming.

This isn't just one of the oldest pies in the book, it's also the easiest. If you think you can't bake, try this one out—you can't screw it up. I think my dog could make this pie, if he wasn't so busy sleeping and eating.

INGREDIENTS

- 4 tablespoons (½ stick) unsalted butter, at room temperature, plus more for the pan
- 4 large eggs
- ¾ cup sugar
- Pinch of salt
- 2 cups whole milk
- 2 teaspoons pure vanilla extract
- ½ cup self-rising flour (I use White Lily)
- Pinch of ground nutmeg

DIRECTIONS

Preheat the oven to 350°F and butter a 9-inch pie pan.

Using an electric mixer, beat the butter, eggs, sugar, salt, milk, vanilla, and flour on medium speed until thick and all the ingredients are incorporated, about 3 minutes. Pour into the pie pan and sprinkle with the nutmeg.

Bake until a crust has fully formed and the pie is golden on top, about 45 minutes. Let cool completely on a wire rack before serving.

MAKES ONE 9-INCH PIE

Nana's apple pie

Every fall, when all the apples were coming in, Nana used to make her famous apple pie. We'd see those apples, and we just knew it was time for her pie. This recipe has been passed around my hometown of Pickens, South Carolina, a million times, from the ladies of the church to the bridge club and, of course, the gossip club. I learned to make this pie when I was six or seven years old, and I still bake one every fall in honor of Nana, from her own handwritten recipe. For some reason, making a double-crust apple pie scares some people, but with Nana's recipe, you've got nothing to fear. I like to use Granny's Easy Butter Crust (page 19) or Nana's Lard Crust (page 20) for this (the lard helps Nana's crust stand up to all that juicy fruit without getting mushy). If you're feeling festive, try Cinnamon Roll Crust (page 24) on the bottom and a regular one on top. Serve with vanilla ice cream or whipped cream.

INGREDIENTS

¾ cup sugar

¼ cup all-purpose flour

½ teaspoon ground cinnamon

½ teaspoon ground nutmeg

Pinch of salt

6 cups thinly sliced peeled apples

2 unbaked 9-inch pie crusts (one in the pan for the bottom and one for the top)

2 tablespoons unsalted butter, cut into small pieces

DIRECTIONS

Preheat the oven to 425°F.

In a large bowl, mix together the sugar, flour, cinnamon, nutmeg, and salt. Stir in the apples and toss until the fruit is completely coated. Pour into the pie crust and dot with the butter. Cover with the top crust and seal the two crusts by pinching the edges together. Cut off excess dough around the edges and cut a few slits in the top crust to let steam escape. Cover the crust edges with foil to avoid burning.

Bake until the crust is browned and juice begins to bubble through the vents, 40 to 50 minutes. Serve hot or at room temperature.

MAKES ONE 9-INCH DOUBLE-CRUST PIE

peaches and cream pie

I first made this a few years ago for a peach contest here in upstate South Carolina, in Gaffney. Peaches and cream are just one of the best combinations ever invented. I like to make this in the late spring/early summer, when the fruit comes in at the orchards right by our house. You can use canned peaches if you're making this in the wintertime, but I like fresh ones best.

INGREDIENTS

pie
- 3 cups sliced peaches
- 1 unbaked 9-inch Granny's Easy Butter Crust (page 19)
- ⅓ cup self-rising flour (I use White Lily)

- 1 cup sugar
- ⅛ teaspoon ground cinnamon
- ⅛ teaspoon salt
- 2 large eggs
- ½ cup sour cream
- ½ teaspoon pure vanilla extract

topping
- ½ cup all-purpose flour
- 1 teaspoon ground cinnamon
- ½ cup sugar
- 4 tablespoons (½ stick) unsalted butter, cold, cut into cubes

DIRECTIONS

Preheat the oven to 350°F.

Start the pie: Put the sliced peaches in the pie crust so they are evenly distributed.

In a small bowl, sift together the flour, sugar, cinnamon, and salt. In a separate bowl, whisk together the eggs, sour cream, and vanilla. Pour half of the flour mixture into the egg mixture and mix well with a wooden spoon. Add the remaining flour mixture to the bowl and mix until smooth. Pour the filling on top of the peaches.

Make the crumb topping: In a bowl, sift together the flour, cinnamon, and sugar. Cut in the butter with a fork or pastry blender until the crumbs are pea-sized. Sprinkle the crumb topping evenly over the pie filling.

Bake until puffed up and golden brown on top, about 1 hour. Let cool completely on a wire rack before serving.

MAKES ONE 9-INCH PIE

BLacKBerry BLow-Ya-away Pie

Pickens, where I live, is the middle of blackberry country, so we eat lots and lots of the berries in summer. One day I had just come back from the grower with a bushel of peaches and 5 gallons of blackberries and this is what happened. I like to use Neufchâtel cream cheese in this because it's sturdier and a little bit sweeter than regular. I always try and use pure extracts, especially in a pie like this, because they just taste so good. This pie's real good with some homemade peach ice cream—now you got me wanting pie and ice cream!

INGREDIENTS

- 2 unbaked 9-inch Nana's Lard Crusts (page 20) or store-bought refrigerated pie crusts
- 1 (8-ounce package) Neufchâtel cream cheese, at room temperature
- 1 cup sugar
- 1 large egg, at room temperature
- 1 teaspoon pure vanilla extract
- 1¼ cups fresh blackberries
- 1½ cups peeled and sliced fresh peaches
- 1½ tablespoons cornstarch
- 1 teaspoon pure almond extract
- 1½ teaspoons ground cinnamon
- 2 tablespoons unsalted butter, melted

DIRECTIONS

Preheat the oven to 375°F.

Press one of the pie crusts into a 9-inch pie pan.

Using an electric mixer, mix together the cream cheese, ¼ cup of the sugar, the egg, and vanilla until creamy. Pour into the pie crust.

In a medium bowl, combine the blackberries and peaches. In a small bowl, mix together the remaining ¾ cup sugar and the cornstarch, then pour the mixture over the fruit, and mix gently. Add the almond extract and 1 teaspoon of the cinnamon and mix gently until the fruit is evenly coated.

Spoon the fruit mixture on top of the cream cheese filling and then place the top crust on top. Press the edges together to seal the top and bottom crusts. Cut off the excess dough around the edges and cut a few slits to let steam escape. Brush the top crust with the melted butter and dust with the remaining ½ teaspoon cinnamon.

Bake until the crust is golden brown, 35 to 40 minutes. Let cool on a wire rack. Serve at room temperature.

MAKES ONE 9-INCH DOUBLE-CRUST PIE

 BLUE RIBBON TIP One thing to remember: The darker your pan, the darker your bake. So, if you're using a glass baking dish, your food will turn out lighter and less brown. If you're using your granny's dark old metal pan, keep an eye on the crust!

WINTER FRUIT PIE

I came up with this for the apple cook-off here in South Carolina, and I only make it when those apples, pears, and cranberries are real fresh—which means wintertime. The mix of all of them here is perfect, especially with that sweet cinnamon-pecan topping. This is an amazing Thanksgiving pie, but I'll make it only if we're hosting dinner. If I'm traveling for the holiday, I don't take it, because I just like it too much to share. If it's at my house, I can keep an eye on it and sneak bites when nobody's looking.

INGREDIENTS ....

filling

- 4 cups thinly sliced peeled baking apples (Granny Smith or Fuji work well)
- ½ cup fresh cranberries
- 2 large firm pears, peeled and thinly sliced
- ⅓ cup plus 2 tablespoons granulated sugar
- 2 teaspoons grated lemon zest

- 1 tablespoon fresh lemon juice
- 1½ tablespoons cornstarch
- ½ teaspoon ground ginger
- ⅛ teaspoon ground nutmeg

- 1 unbaked 10-inch deep-dish pie crust (such as Nana's Lard Crust [page 20] or Granny's Easy Butter Crust [page 19]), chilled

topping

- ¾ cup whole-wheat or all-purpose flour
- ½ cup firmly packed light brown sugar
- ½ cup pecan halves
- ¼ teaspoon ground cinnamon
- 3 tablespoons unsalted butter, cold, cut into small pieces
- 1½ tablespoons whole milk

DIRECTIONS ....

Make the filling: Combine the apples, cranberries, pears, ⅓ cup of the granulated sugar, the lemon zest, and lemon juice in a large bowl. Toss to coat the fruit. Set aside for 10 minutes.

Preheat the oven to 400°F.

Mix the remaining 2 tablespoons sugar, the cornstarch, ginger, and nutmeg in a small bowl. Add to the fruit and toss well to combine. Scrape the filling into the pie crust.

Bake for 30 minutes. Cover the edges of the pie crust loosely with foil to prevent burning and bake for 10 minutes more.

recipe continues

Meanwhile, prepare the topping: Combine the flour, brown sugar, pecans, and cinnamon in a food processor and pulse 5 or 6 times to chop the nuts. Scatter the butter over the dry ingredients. Pulse again until the butter is chopped into fine pieces. With the processor running, add the milk in a thin stream and stop as soon as it has all been added. Empty the mixture into a bowl and gently rub it between your fingers until it looks and feels a little like damp sand.

After the pie has been in the oven for 40 minutes, reduce the oven temperature to 350°F. Remove the pie from the oven and set it on a baking sheet. Spread the crumb topping evenly over the fruit, patting down gently. Bake the pie until the fruit is tender when pierced with the tip of a knife and you can see the juices bubbling at the edges, 20 to 30 minutes more. Keep a close eye on the topping: Once it starts to brown, lay a large sheet of foil over the pie to prevent any further darkening.

Let cool on a wire rack for at least 1 hour before serving.

MAKES ONE 10-INCH DEEP-DISH PIE

saraBlake's "Punkin" Pie

This is a great Thanksgiving pie—or, in my case, year-round pie, because my daughter, Sarablake, just loves anything to do with pumpkin. Down here, when the holidays are over, you can buy puréed pumpkin for a quarter a can, so that's when I stock up and then make pumpkin desserts all winter long. The filling is just plain ol' regular pumpkin, but I put a praline glaze over it because I like mixing things up. You can use any pie crust you like, but I just love making this one with my cinnamon roll crust. The cinnamon and pumpkin go together real good.

INGREDIENTS

- 2 large eggs
- 1 cup plus 2 tablespoons firmly packed light brown sugar
- 1½ teaspoons ground cinnamon
- 1 teaspoon ground nutmeg
- 1 teaspoon pure vanilla extract
- 1 (15-ounce) can pure pumpkin puree
- 1 (12-ounce) can evaporated milk
- 1 unbaked 9-inch Cinnamon Roll Crust (page 24)
- 1 tablespoon unsalted butter, melted
- ½ cup pecans, finely chopped

DIRECTIONS

Preheat the oven to 425°F.

Whip the eggs with a whisk until blended. Whisk in 1 cup of the brown sugar, the cinnamon, nutmeg, and vanilla extract. Then mix in the pumpkin puree and evaporated milk until thoroughly incorporated. Pour the pumpkin mixture into the pie crust.

Bake for 15 minutes. Reduce the oven temperature to 325°F and bake until the filling is set in the center, another 40 to 50 minutes.

To make the praline glaze, stir together the remaining 2 tablespoons brown sugar and the melted butter and then add the pecans.

Pour the glaze on top of the pie and return to the oven until the brown sugar is melted into the top of the pie, about 5 minutes.

Let cool and then refrigerate for at least 3 hours or overnight before serving.

MAKES ONE 9-INCH PIE

chapter
2

COOKIES
& Bars

BEST-EVER CHOCOLATE
CHIP COOKIES

SLAP-YA-MAMA FUDGE
COOKIES

REDNECK DANISH COOKIES
FOR A CROWD

MIRACLE WHIP PUMPKIN BARS

CLASSIC SOUTHERN LEMON
BARS

CHOCOLATE CHIP PUMPKIN
COOKIES

DOUBLE-CHOCOLATE
COOKIE BARS

COW PATTIES

PLAIN OL' PEANUT BUTTER
COOKIES

TEXAS-SIZED GINGERSNAPS

TEA COOKIES

ICED OATMEAL COOKIES

NANA'S CHRISTMAS SUGAR
COOKIES

EGGNOG COOKIES

ALMOND BARS

PUMPKIN "BROWNIE" BARS

CHEESECAKE-CHOCOLATE
CHIP COOKIE BARS

Best-ever chocolate Chip cookies

If you're going to be a baker, you better have a real good chocolate chip cookie recipe. I tried everything from Nestlé Toll House to Hershey's, forty recipes or more, and didn't like any of them—too moist or too dry, never just right. My ideal cookie's got a cake-type feel to it—puffy and thick and crisp on the bottom. After years of playing around in the kitchen and a whole lot of trial and error, I got this one—my perfect best-ever chocolate chip cookie—not adapted from nowhere!

I buy self-rising flour, because I think to myself, "Why buy all those extra ingredients, especially if you know your baking soda is going to go bad soon?" If you don't have a mixer, go ahead and use a whisk. Just make sure all that sugar starts to melt in the hot butter; you want this real smooth before you go on putting in anything else. I use a cookie scoop when I plop these down on the baking sheets, so they're all the same size; if you use a spoon, pay attention to the sizing.

INGREDIENTS

¾ cup (1½ sticks) unsalted butter, melted, plus more for the baking sheets

1 cup firmly packed light brown sugar

½ cup granulated sugar

1 teaspoon pure vanilla extract

2 large eggs

2½ cups self-rising flour (I use White Lily)

2 cups semisweet chocolate chips

 BLUE RIBBON TIP These cookies are good by themselves, but if you feel like adding anything, go ahead—the dough can take it. I like to put in nuts or M&M's or sometimes switch up the chocolate chips to mint chocolate, peanut butter, or toffee chips.

Preheat the oven to 325°F. Lightly grease 2 or 3 baking sheets.

Using an electric mixer, beat the butter, brown sugar, and granulated sugar on low speed until fully blended. Add the vanilla extract and eggs and continue mixing until combined. Sift the flour into the bowl and mix until just incorporated. Stir in the chocolate chips by hand with a wooden spoon.

Drop rounded tablespoon-and-a-half-sized balls of dough onto the baking sheets, leaving 2-inch gaps between the balls. Bake until lightly browned around the edges, 15 to 19 minutes. Transfer to a wire rack to cool completely. Store in an airtight container.

Makes about 3 dozen cookies

SLaP-Ya-MaMa FuDGe COOKIeS

I probably make around five hundred of these suckers a year to put in Christmas baskets, because nobody wants presents from me—they just want baked goods. Why the title? These cookies are so doggone good, you'd slap your mama to get the last one! They've got everything you're looking for: a deep, rich chocolate flavor; crunchy-sweet nuts; smooth white chocolate; and, if you're using it, a touch of chipotle heat to hit the back of your throat at the end. These cookies are crunchy on the outside and chewy on the inside. I know they have a lot of steps, but they're easier to make than you think, and worth the effort—I promise!

INGREDIENTS

1 cup pecans or walnuts

½ cup self-rising flour (I use White Lily)

Pinch of salt

1 teaspoon espresso powder

1½ teaspoons chipotle powder (optional)

1 pound semisweet chocolate, coarsely chopped

4 tablespoons (½ stick) unsalted butter, cut into small chunks

1¾ cups sugar

4 large eggs, at room temperature

1 teaspoon pure vanilla extract

1 cup dark chocolate chips

1 cup white chocolate chips

DIRECTIONS

Preheat the oven to 350°F.

Spread out the nuts on a baking sheet and toast in the oven until lightly browned and fragrant, 8 to 10 minutes. Let cool and then chop coarsely. Leave the oven on.

Whisk together the flour, salt, espresso powder, and chipotle powder, if using.

Melt the semisweet chocolate and the butter in the microwave or in a stainless-steel bowl placed over a saucepan of simmering water, stirring until smooth. Remove from the heat and set aside to cool to room temperature.

Using an electric mixer, beat the sugar and eggs until pale yellow and thick, about 5 minutes. Beat in the melted chocolate mixture and vanilla extract. Gently fold in the flour mixture until just incorporated. Do not overmix. Stir in the dark and white chocolate chips and the nuts. Cover with plastic wrap and refrigerate until just firm, 30 to 60 minutes.

Line 2 baking sheets with parchment paper and drop the dough by rounded tablespoons onto the paper, leaving 2 inches between each cookie. Bake until puffy and cracked on top, 14 to 16 minutes.

Remove from the oven and set the baking sheets on wire racks to cool until the cookies are just firm, 10 minutes. Remove the cookies from the baking sheets and let cool completely on the racks. Store in an airtight container.

Makes about 18 big cookies

 Blue Ribbon Tip I'm a firm believer in espresso powder— if you use it with chocolate, it just jacks up that flavor, without making it all coffee tasting. It's a real sister to chocolate and I use it all the time.

redneck Danish cookies for a crowd

Pickens ain't a rich community, and when we can cook or bake something for our family and friends without spending a fortune, it's always a good thing. Not so long ago a friend of mine came to me and said, "Frannie, I'm having a bridal shower and I want those fancy, tasty Danish wedding cookies, but I honestly can't afford to buy them for a hundred people." So I created a recipe that has the same flavor and the same look using cake mix, which is cheaper than combining flour, butter, and sugar. I don't normally use much cake mix, so at the grocery store everyone was asking me, "What the heck are you doing with all that cake mix?" I just told them I was working on something. These cookies are rich, but you don't gotta be to make them!

INGREDIENTS

- ½ cup shortening (I use Crisco)
- 1 teaspoon butter rum extract
- 1 large egg
- 1 (15-ounce) box classic white cake mix
- ¾ cup chopped peanuts
- ½ cup chopped dark chocolate (any kind)
- 1 cup confectioner's sugar

DIRECTIONS

Preheat the oven to 375°F.

Using an electric mixer, combine the shortening, ¼ cup water, the butter rum extract, and egg until fully blended; the mixture will look lumpy and wet. Add the cake mix and continue to mix until smooth. Stir in the peanuts and chocolate by hand using a wooden spoon.

Drop by rounded tablespoons onto ungreased baking sheets and bake until deep tan in color, but not brown, about 12 minutes.

Remove the cookies from the oven, and while hot, press the tops of the cookies into the confectioner's sugar. Flip back over, and let cool completely, right side up, on wire racks. Store in an airtight container.

MAKES ABOUT 100 COOKIES

MIRACLE WHIP PUMPKIN BARS

Down here, we're serious about our mayonnaise. Duke's mayonnaise is made right in town, and I've lived my whole life using nothing else. When my husband and I first got married, we were at the grocery store and he put Miracle Whip in the buggy. So I asked what the heck he was doing. He's from North Carolina, so I couldn't blame him—but I could change him. Soon after I was prepping for a pumpkin cook-off and trying to use whatever I could find in our kitchen. I found that jar of Miracle Whip, threw some in with the pumpkin, and ended up winning the whole dang competition! After a lot of years together, my husband's now trained to go for the Duke's, except for when I'm making this recipe. . . . The Miracle Whip acts as a binding agent in the bars, and since it's sweeter and thinner than regular mayonnaise, the taste blends in and leaves these light and dense at the same time.

INGREDIENTS

Nonstick cooking spray

1 (15-ounce) box spice cake mix

1 (15-ounce) can pure pumpkin puree

3 large eggs

½ cup chopped walnuts or pecans (optional)

1 teaspoon pure vanilla extract

1 cup Miracle Whip

1 cup confectioner's sugar

2 tablespoons heavy cream, half-and-half, whole milk, or even flavored coffee creamer

DIRECTIONS

Preheat the oven to 350°F. Spray a 9 × 13-inch pan with cooking spray.

In a large bowl, combine the cake mix, pumpkin, eggs, nuts (if using), vanilla, and Miracle Whip and mix with a wooden spoon until fully blended. Pour into the pan and bake until a cake tester or toothpick inserted into the center comes out clean, 30 to 35 minutes. Let cool completely on a wire rack.

Mix together the confectioner's sugar and heavy cream until smooth. Pour the glaze on top of the cake. Let set before cutting into 12 bars. Store in an airtight container.

MAKES 12 BARS

Classic Southern Lemon Bars

Lemon bars are a classic Southern treat, and I've been eating them as long as I've been eating. This is the recipe I grew up on, and I found it in Nana's recipe book, or, as we call it around here, "The Bible." My kids just love them and so do I—nothing like that fresh lemony sour-sweet flavor. This is a real summertime recipe, perfect for porch sitting with a big glass of sweet tea. Nothing goes better with tea than lemon.

INGREDIENTS

crust
- ½ cup (1 stick) unsalted butter, at room temperature, plus more for the pan
- 1½ cups all-purpose flour
- ⅓ cup granulated sugar
- ¼ teaspoon salt
- 1 tablespoon grated lemon zest

filling
- 4 large eggs
- 1⅓ cups granulated sugar
- 1 cup strained fresh lemon juice

Confectioner's sugar

DIRECTIONS

Preheat the oven to 350°F. Line a 9-inch square pan with parchment paper and then grease with butter.

Make the crust: Using an electric mixer, combine the flour, granulated sugar, salt, and lemon zest. Cut the ½ cup butter into chunks and add to the bowl. Blend on low speed until the mixture forms coarse, sandy crumbs. Pour into the pan and press the mixture down into an even layer. Bake until just lightly browned around the edges, 16 to 19 minutes.

While the crust is baking, prepare the filling: In a large bowl, whisk together the eggs, granulated sugar, and lemon juice.

Pour the filling into the baked crust while the crust is still hot. Bake until the filling is set and doesn't jiggle when the pan is gently shaken, about 20 minutes. Let cool completely on a wire rack before dusting with confectioner's sugar and slicing into 9 bars. Store in an airtight container.

MAKES 9 BARS

CHOCOLATE CHIP PUMPKIN COOKIES

This is a simple cookie, real good and light—it ain't going to stop a war or anything, but it'll sure brighten your day, especially if you make them in the dead of summer, when you're just waiting on fall to come.

INGREDIENTS

- ½ cup (1 stick) unsalted butter, at room temperature
- 1½ cups sugar
- 1 large egg
- 1 cup pure pumpkin puree
- 1 teaspoon pure vanilla extract
- 1 teaspoon ground cinnamon
- 1 teaspoon ground allspice
- 2½ cups cake flour (see Blue Ribbon Tip, below)
- 1 teaspoon baking powder
- 1 teaspoon baking soda
- ½ teaspoon salt
- 1 cup semisweet chocolate chips

DIRECTIONS

Preheat the oven to 350°F. Line 2 or 3 baking sheets with parchment paper or silicone baking mats.

Using an electric mixer, beat the butter and sugar together, scraping down the sides of the bowl, until smooth, about 2 minutes. Add the egg, pumpkin, vanilla extract, cinnamon, and allspice. Continue mixing for 2 additional minutes and scrape down the sides of the bowl again.

Add the flour, baking powder, baking soda, and salt to the bowl, and mix just until the flour is incorporated. Stir in the chocolate chips, using a wooden spoon.

Using a 1½-tablespoon cookie scoop (or a spoon), scoop the dough, placing about 2 inches apart on the baking sheets. Bake until puffy and orangey golden-brown, about 10 minutes. Transfer to wire racks to cool completely. Store in an airtight container.

MAKES ABOUT 30 COOKIES

 BLUE RIBBON TIP If you don't have cake flour, just make your own: For every cup of all-purpose flour, scoop out 2 tablespoons and replace with 2 tablespoons cornstarch.

DOUBLE-CHOCOLATE COOKIE BARS

People talk about tasting the love in food, and it's something I know to be true. Growing up, I was always either at Nana's or Granny's house—because my house was smack dab in the middle. Nana would bake up a treat for us when we visited; you knew you were loved when Nana was making you something. She made these bars for us all the time, and I'll keep on making them forever. The recipe is simple as all get-out—you don't even need an oven for it!—and the chocolate–peanut butter combination is a classic. Just don't ask me why there's condensed milk in the recipe; when it comes to Nana's recipes, I don't question them, because they always work.

INGREDIENTS

- ½ cup (1 stick) unsalted butter, at room temperature
- ¾ cup firmly packed light brown sugar
- 1 teaspoon pure vanilla extract
- 2 cups all-purpose flour
- 1 (14-ounce) can sweetened condensed milk
- 2 cups mini semisweet chocolate chips
- ½ cup creamy peanut butter (I use Jif)
- ½ cup milk chocolate chips

DIRECTIONS

Line an 8-inch square pan with parchment paper.

Using an electric mixer, mix together the butter and brown sugar until fluffy, about 3 minutes. Add the vanilla extract and beat until combined.

Turn the mixer to low and alternate adding portions of the flour with portions of the condensed milk until both ingredients are fully combined. Gently fold in the mini semisweet chocolate chips. Press into the pan.

The mixture will be sticky so lightly flour your hands if needed. Cover with plastic wrap and refrigerate until firm, at least 3 hours or overnight.

Melt the peanut butter and milk chocolate chips in the microwave or in a double boiler. Pour over the cold bars and spread evenly. Refrigerate until firm, at least 1 hour, before cutting into 8 bars. Store in an airtight container.

MAKES 8 BARS

COW PATTIES

This is one old recipe—a hundred years or more! Up north they call them "No-Bake Chocolate Cookies," but down here, we call them "Cow Patties." I can't tell you who invented them, but thank God they did—they're my all-time favorite cookies. Millions of people make this recipe or some version of it because they are real simple and take just 10 minutes to throw together. And most of that time's just getting your ingredients in order! You can't screw these up except for one way: You cannot make Cow Patties on a humid day; they just will not work. I think margarine works better in these cookies, but you can use unsalted butter, if you like. I like slightly salty peanut butter for these, but if you prefer unsalted, try that. Use what you've got, people!

INGREDIENTS

2 cups sugar

3 tablespoons unsweetened cocoa powder

½ cup whole milk

½ cup (1 stick) margarine

½ cup creamy peanut butter (I use Jif)

1 teaspoon pure vanilla extract

Pinch of salt

3 cups quick-cooking rolled oats

DIRECTIONS

Line 2 or 3 baking sheets with wax paper.

Combine the sugar, cocoa powder, milk, and margarine in a large saucepan. Over medium heat, bring to a rolling boil and continue to boil for 1 full minute. Add the peanut butter. Remove from the heat and then add the vanilla, salt, and oats. Stir well. Let cool slightly.

Drop the mixture by rounded tablespoons onto the baking sheets. Let sit until firm, about 1 hour. Store in an airtight container.

MAKES ABOUT 3 DOZEN COOKIES

PLaIn OL' Peanut butter cookies

The only thing my family loves as much as pumpkin is peanut butter! We just can't get enough, and, yes, we eat it straight out of the jar with a spoon. You can put any kind of peanut butter you like in these—I usually go with the creamy kind of salty kind, but it's up to you. When you're about to cook them, make sure the baking sheets are *not* greased—or the cookies will spread too much in the oven and start to burn. This is Granny's recipe.

INGREDIENTS

- 1¼ cups all-purpose flour
- ¾ tablespoon ground cinnamon
- ¾ teaspoon baking soda
- ½ teaspoon baking powder
- ¼ teaspoon salt
- ½ cup (1 stick) unsalted butter, at room temperature
- ½ cup granulated sugar
- ½ cup firmly packed light brown sugar
- ½ cup creamy peanut butter (I use Jif)
- 1 large egg
- 1 teaspoon pure vanilla extract

DIRECTIONS

In a medium bowl, whisk together the flour, cinnamon, baking soda, baking powder, and salt. Using an electric mixer, beat the butter, granulated sugar, brown sugar, peanut butter, egg, and vanilla on medium speed until well blended, about 2 minutes. Gradually beat in the flour mixture on low speed until mixed. Refrigerate the dough until firm, about 2 hours.

Preheat the oven to 375°F.

Shape the dough into 1-inch balls. Place the balls about 3 inches apart on ungreased baking sheets. Gently flatten with fork tines, pressing a crisscross pattern onto the tops of the cookies. Bake until lightly browned, 8 to 10 minutes. Let cool on the baking sheets for 1 minute, then transfer to wire racks, and let cool completely. Store in an airtight container.

Makes about 26 cookies

Texas-Sized Gingersnaps

You just gotta have gingersnaps when the holidays come around. Chewy, crisp around the edges, and a little spicy—*and* they make the kitchen smell like heaven. These were one of Daddy's favorites, and I liked to make them for him whenever I got the chance. These are real big and round and look pretty on a tray at the treats table at Christmastime.

INGREDIENTS

- 2½ cups all-purpose flour
- 2¼ teaspoons baking soda
- ½ teaspoon salt
- 2 tablespoons ground ginger
- ½ teaspoon ground allspice
- ¾ cup (1½ sticks) unsalted butter, at room temperature
- ½ cup firmly packed light brown sugar
- ¾ cup granulated sugar
- ¼ cup plus 2 tablespoons dark molasses
- 1 large egg

DIRECTIONS

Preheat the oven to 350°F. Line 3 baking sheets with parchment paper.

In a medium bowl, whisk together the flour, baking soda, salt, ginger, and allspice.

Using an electric mixer, beat together the butter, brown sugar, and ½ cup of the granulated sugar until light and fluffy. Blend in the molasses and egg. With the mixer on low speed, add the flour mixture and beat until just combined.

Divide the dough into 12 equal balls. Put the remaining ¼ cup granulated sugar in a bowl and roll the balls in the sugar. Place the balls 4 inches apart on the baking sheets. Flatten with the bottom of a glass or your hands into 3-inch rounds. Sprinkle the tops of the cookies with the remaining sugar in the bowl.

Bake until browned, 12 to 15 minutes, rotating the sheets midway through baking. If more than one baking sheet is in the oven at a time, switch the top and bottom sheets midway through baking. Transfer to wire racks to cool completely. Store in an airtight container.

Makes About 12 Large Cookies

Tea Cookies

Growing up, Granny and Nana would tell me, "A Southern lady always knows how to make a tea cookie." This here's Nana's recipe, and the best one I ever tried. Round here, when we don't want to act like rednecks, we eat some tea cookies and sip on tea, pinkies up—all proper-like. Some good old-fashioned Southern etiquette, or, as I say, "Southern belle–type crap." But it is a real Southern tradition to sit on the porch, gossip, have some sweet tea, and munch on these little crunchy treats.

INGREDIENTS

- 4¼ cups all-purpose flour
- 1 teaspoon baking soda
- 1 teaspoon cream of tartar
- ½ teaspoon salt
- 1¼ cups granulated sugar
- 1 cup confectioner's sugar
- 1 cup (2 sticks) unsalted butter, at room temperature
- ¾ cup vegetable oil
- 2 tablespoons whole milk or heavy cream
- 1 tablespoon pure vanilla extract
- 2 large eggs

DIRECTIONS

In a bowl, whisk together the flour, baking soda, cream of tartar, and salt. Using an electric mixer, beat together 1 cup of the granulated sugar, the confectioner's sugar, butter, oil, milk, vanilla, and eggs. Add the flour mixture and mix until just combined. Cover and chill until firm, about 2 hours.

Preheat the oven to 350°F.

Form the dough into 1-inch balls and roll in the remaining ¼ cup granulated sugar. Place the balls 3 inches apart on ungreased baking sheets. Flatten each ball to ¼ inch thick with the bottom of a glass and then sprinkle the tops with the remaining sugar in the bowl.

Bake until the edges of the cookies begin to turn golden brown, 13 to 15 minutes. Remove the cookies from the baking sheet and let cool completely on wire racks. Store in an airtight container.

MAKES ABOUT 3½ DOZEN COOKIES

ICED OATMEAL COOKIES

This here's another classic cookie, and one y'all should learn how to make. I think oatmeal's an underrated ingredient and it makes such a dang good cookie! This is another recipe I found in Nana's book, written on the back of an envelope; I bet it was passed around by the ladies of the church during preaching. I like these in the wintertime. Make sure you notice, the butter to use here is salted, but if you only got unsalted, it ain't the end of the world; just add an extra pinch of salt to the dough.

INGREDIENTS ....

- 1½ cups old-fashioned rolled oats
- 2 cups all-purpose flour
- 2 teaspoons baking powder
- ½ teaspoon baking soda
- ½ teaspoon salt
- 1½ teaspoons ground cinnamon
- ½ teaspoon ground nutmeg
- 1 cup (2 sticks) salted butter, at room temperature
- ¾ cup granulated sugar
- ¾ cup firmly packed light brown sugar
- 2 large eggs
- 2 teaspoons pure vanilla extract
- 2 cups confectioner's sugar
- 3 tablespoons whole milk

DIRECTIONS ....

Preheat the oven to 350°F. Line 2 or 3 baking sheets with parchment paper.

Pour the oats into a food processor and pulse until partially ground, about 15 seconds. In a mixing bowl, whisk together the ground outs, flour, baking powder, baking soda, salt, cinnamon, and nutmeg.

Using an electric mixer, beat the butter, granulated sugar, and light brown sugar on medium-high speed until pale and fluffy, 3 to 4 minutes. Add the eggs, one at a time, mixing until combined after each addition. Stir in the vanilla extract. With the mixer on low speed, slowly add the flour mixture and mix just until combined, scraping the bottom and sides of the bowl as needed. Let the cookie dough rest for 10 minutes at room temperature.

Scoop the dough out about 2 tablespoons at a time and drop onto the baking sheets, leaving 2 inches between each cookie. Bake until browned, 11 to 15 minutes. Let the cookies rest on the baking sheets for a few minutes before transferring to wire racks to cool completely.

In a bowl, whisk together the confectioner's sugar and milk until smooth. Dip the tops of the cooled cookies in the icing, allowing the excess to run off. Return to the racks to allow the icing to set. Store in an airtight container.

MAKES ABOUT 3 DOZEN COOKIES

nana's christmas sugar cookies

As you can tell, my Nana and I were real close. Every time I get out her recipe book and bake for family or friends, I think of her. It makes every cookie, cake, or pie even more special. Every Thanksgiving my Mama's family, which was a big family, would draw names for gifts and then we'd exchange them on Christmas Eve. We'd gather at Nana's house, so a few days before, I'd go over there to bake with her—and these cookies always made the list. They have a lot of ingredients, but they turn out perfect, and they look perfect, too. I looked forward to that time with my Nana every single year—it brings back memories thinking about it, and I hope you make memories with this recipe, too.

INGREDIENTS

- 4 cups all-purpose flour
- 1 teaspoon baking soda
- 1 teaspoon cream of tartar
- ½ teaspoon salt
- 1 cup confectioner's sugar

- 1 cup granulated sugar
- 1 cup vegetable oil
- 1 cup (2 sticks) unsalted butter or margarine, plus more for the baking sheets

- 2 large eggs
- 1 teaspoon pure vanilla extract
- About ⅓ cup colored sugar

DIRECTIONS

In a bowl, whisk together the flour, baking soda, cream of tartar, and salt. Using an electric mixer, beat the confectioner's sugar, granulated sugar, oil, and butter until fluffy. Beat in the eggs and vanilla. Add the flour mixture and mix until just combined. Cover with plastic wrap and refrigerate for 1 hour.

Preheat the oven to 350°F. Lightly grease 2 or 3 baking sheets.

Form the dough into 1-inch balls with your hands and place on the baking sheets, leaving 2 inches between the cookies. Press each ball flat with the bottom of a glass or your hands and then sprinkle with colored sugar.

Bake until golden brown around the edges, 12 to 15 minutes. Transfer to wire racks and let cool completely. Store in an airtight container.

MAKES ABOUT 3 DOZEN COOKIES

 SAVORY TEA COOKIES I always add a different flavor to this dough such, as a touch of cinnamon, or, if you're feeling adventuresome, add ½ teaspoon each finely chopped rosemary and basil to make a savory tea cookie that can be served as a side to a spread at your next party. Omit the colored sugar topping.

 BLUE RIBBON TIPS This dough can be rolled out and cut with cookie cutters, if you like. Just make sure not to overwork the dough.

Before the holiday madness sets in, you can make a big batch of this dough, wrap it well in plastic wrap, and freeze for up three months in an airtight container. Defrost overnight in the refrigerator before shaping and baking.

eggnog cookies

I love, love, love eggnog. I'd drink it year-round if they made it, but it's so doggone heavy, they don't sell it in the summertime. I first made these for a Christmas gathering ten or twelve years ago, and when I tried them, I knew the recipe was going to be one to hang on to. Now, most times with eggnog, people either love it or hate it. But even the folks who don't like eggnog love these cookies. The flavor's not too overpowering, but it sure is there. This is one of my favorite wintertime cookies, especially with a mug of hot spiced cider or coffee.

INGREDIENTS

cookies

2¼ cups all-purpose flour

1 teaspoon baking powder

½ teaspoon ground cinnamon

½ teaspoon ground nutmeg

1¼ cups granulated sugar

¾ cup (1½ sticks) salted butter, at room temperature

½ cup eggnog

2 large egg yolks

1 teaspoon pure vanilla extract

icing

3 cups confectioner's sugar

4 tablespoons (½ stick) unsalted butter, at room temperature

About ½ cup eggnog

1 tablespoon ground nutmeg (optional)

DIRECTIONS

Preheat the oven to 300°F. Line 2 or 3 baking sheets with parchment paper.

Make the cookies: In a medium bowl, whisk together the flour, baking powder, cinnamon, and nutmeg. Using an electric mixer, beat the granulated sugar and salted butter until fluffy, about 4 minutes. Add the eggnog, egg yolks, and vanilla extract and beat on medium speed until smooth. Add the

flour mixture and beat on low speed until just combined.

Drop the dough by rounded teaspoons onto the baking sheets, 1 inch apart. Bake until the bottoms turn light brown, 21 to 24 minutes. Immediately transfer the cookies to wire racks using a spatula and let cool completely.

Prepare the icing: Using an electric mixer, beat the confectioner's sugar and unsalted butter until well blended. Gradually beat in the eggnog until the icing is smooth. You may need more or less eggnog depending on the consistency you like. Frost the cooled cookies and, if desired, sprinkle lightly with the nutmeg using a sifter or strainer. Let the icing set before serving. Store in an airtight container.

MAKES ABOUT 3 DOZEN COOKIES

ALMOND BARS

Almond will never be my go-to flavor, but when Granny used to make these for Thanksgiving, I couldn't stop eating them. The holidays were when Granny would pull out the big guns, and these bars—with their deep almond flavor and nice fluffy meringue topping—always made the cut.

INGREDIENTS

bars
- 1½ cups (3 sticks) unsalted butter or shortening (I use Crisco), plus more for the pan
- 2 large egg yolks
- ¾ cup granulated sugar
- ¼ teaspoon pure almond extract
- 1¼ cups cake flour
- 1 teaspoon baking powder
- ½ teaspoon salt

topping
- 1 large egg white
- 1 cup firmly packed light brown sugar, sifted
- 1 cup slivered almonds

DIRECTIONS

Preheat the oven to 325°F. Grease a 7 × 11-inch baking pan.

Make the bars: Using an electric mixer, beat the egg yolks until light and fluffy. Next use the mixer to beat the butter and granulated sugar together until light and fluffy. Add the egg yolks and the almond extract to the butter mixture and mix until combined.

In a separate bowl, sift together the flour, baking powder, and salt. Mix half of the flour mixture into the butter mixture, then add 2 tablespoons water, and finally mix in the remaining flour mixture. Pour into the pan and smooth the top.

Bake until a cake tester or toothpick inserted into the center comes out clean, about 30 minutes. Let cool slightly while you prepare the meringue topping. Keep the oven on.

Whip the topping: Using an electric mixer, beat the egg white until stiff. Use a rubber spatula to fold in the brown sugar. Spread over the bars and sprinkle the almonds on top. Return to the oven and bake until golden peaks form on top, 8 to 10 minutes. Let cool completely on a wire rack before cutting into 15 bars. Store in an airtight container in the fridge.

MAKES ABOUT 15 BARS

PUMPKIN "Brownie" Bars

My whole family just loves pumpkin—matter of fact, we eat it year-round. One day, instead of making the same old pumpkin pie or pumpkin spice cake, I was playing around in the kitchen and came up with this total fluke of a recipe. These bars are just so good, and the cream cheese topping makes them even better and richer. These make for a great Halloween treat!

INGREDIENTS

bars
- 1 cup vegetable oil, plus more for the pan
- 1 (15-ounce) can pure pumpkin puree
- 4 large eggs
- 1 teaspoon pure vanilla extract
- 2 cups self-rising flour (I use White Lily)
- 2 cups granulated sugar
- 1 teaspoon pumpkin spice mix

topping
- 1 (8-ounce) package cream cheese, at room temperature
- 5 tablespoons unsalted butter, at room temperature
- 1⅓ cups confectioner's sugar
- 1 teaspoon ground cinnamon
- ½ cup chopped walnuts

DIRECTIONS

Preheat the oven to 350°F. Grease an 8-inch square pan with oil.

Make the bars: Using an electric mixer, mix the pumpkin, eggs, oil, and vanilla extract. In a smaller bowl, stir together the flour, granulated sugar, and pumpkin spice mix. Add the flour mixture to the pumpkin mixture and mix until combined. Do not overmix.

Pour the batter into the pan and bake until the edges have browned and the middle springs back when touched, about 40 minutes. Remove from the oven and let cool completely on a wire rack.

Prepare the topping: Beat the cream cheese and butter in a large bowl until fluffy. Add the confectioner's sugar and continue mixing until smooth. Mix in the cinnamon.

Spread the cream cheese topping over the bars, sprinkle with the nuts, and serve, cutting into 12 bars. Store in an airtight container in the fridge.

MaKes 12 Bars

cheesecake-chocolate chip cookie bars

Me and Mama came up with this recipe to put two of my favorite things together: cheesecake and chocolate chip cookies. I first made these for a group of ladies, and they were a hit—the women couldn't get enough. That was twenty-some years ago! This recipe just has to be shared, so here you go—one of my absolute favorites. These are a real impressive bar—rich, cakey, and chewy.

INGREDIENTS

cookies
- ¾ cup (1½ sticks) unsalted butter, melted, plus more for the pan
- 1 cup firmly packed light brown sugar
- ½ cup granulated sugar
- 1 large egg
- 1 large egg yolk
- 2 teaspoons pure vanilla extract
- 2⅛ cups all-purpose flour
- ½ teaspoon salt
- ½ teaspoon baking soda
- 2 cups semisweet chocolate chips (from one 12-ounce bag)

filling
- 1 (8-ounce) package cream cheese, at room temperature
- ½ cup confectioner's sugar
- 1 large egg
- ½ teaspoon pure vanilla extract

DIRECTIONS

Preheat the oven to 350°F. Butter a 9 × 13-inch pan.

Make the cookies: In a large bowl, whisk together the butter, brown sugar, and granulated sugar. Add the egg, egg yolk, and vanilla and mix well. Switch to a rubber spatula and fold in the flour, salt, and baking soda; do not overmix. Fold in the chocolate chips until combined.

Use lightly moistened hands to press half of the dough evenly onto the bottom of the prepared pan; it will be a thin layer. Fill in any holes with additional cookie dough.

Make the filling: Using an electric mixer, beat the cream cheese and confectioner's sugar on medium-high speed until light and fluffy, 1 to 2 minutes. Add the egg and vanilla and mix until well combined. Spread the cheesecake filling over the layer of cookie dough in the pan.

Using your hands, flatten tablespoon-sized balls of the remaining cookie dough into flat rounds that are ⅛ to ¼ inch thick. Arrange these rounds over the top of the cheesecake layer, pressing very lightly to adhere them to the cheesecake layer. It's okay if there are small spaces; the entire top doesn't need to be completely covered as long as it is mostly covered with cookie dough.

Bake until very lightly browned on the edges, 35 to 40 minutes. Let cool completely on a wire rack. Refrigerate until chilled, 1 to 2 hours. Cut into 24 squares. Store in an airtight container in the fridge.

MAKES 24 SMALL BARS

chapter 3

cakes
LIKE GRANNY MADE

Nana's iced pound cake

Baked goods just bring everyone together, and you can't get more comforting than a pound cake—it's a standard down here. If there's a gathering, whether a funeral or a church function, there's always some kind of pound cake on the table. This here is Nana's recipe; it's probably a hundred years old. She made it with all lard, but over the years, I changed it to shortening and butter together, which makes it lighter. The glaze is a real simple topping you can use for any plain cake. This is as simple to make as it is to eat.

INGREDIENTS

cake
- 1 cup (2 sticks) unsalted butter, at room temperature, plus more for the pan
- ½ cup shortening (I use Crisco)
- 3 cups granulated sugar
- 5 large eggs

- ¼ cup whole milk
- ½ cup sour cream
- 2 teaspoons vanilla butter and nut flavoring (see Blue Ribbon Tip, opposite)
- 3 cups self-rising flour (I use White Lily), sifted

glaze (optional)
- 2 cups confectioner's sugar
- 1 teaspoon pure vanilla extract
- 3 tablespoons whole milk

DIRECTIONS

Preheat the oven to 325°F. Grease a 10-inch Bundt pan.

Make the cake: Using an electric mixer, beat the butter, shortening, and granulated sugar until smooth and pale. Add the eggs, one at a time, mixing well after each addition. Whisk together the milk, sour cream, and vanilla butter and nut flavoring. Alternate adding the flour and the milk mixture, starting and ending with the flour, and mixing until just combined; do not overmix.

Pour the batter into the pan and bake until golden brown and a cake tester or toothpick inserted into the center of the cake comes out clean, about 1 hour 15 minutes. Let cool in the pan on a wire rack for 15 minutes before inverting the cake onto the rack and removing the pan. Let cool completely.

Mix the glaze: Whisk together the confectioner's sugar, vanilla extract, and milk until smooth. Pour over the cake and let set before serving.

Makes one 10-inch bundt cake

 Praline Pound Cake Make a toasted pecan and brown sugar glaze to pour on top instead of Nana's glaze: In a medium saucepan, combine 4 tablespoons (½ stick) unsalted butter, 1 cup sugar, and 1 cup toasted chopped pecans. Cook over medium heat until thickened, about 10 minutes. Carefully add ¼ cup heavy cream and stir until you have a glaze. Pour over the cooled cake and let set before serving.

 Blue Ribbon Tip In the summertime, I replace the vanilla butter and nut flavoring with lemon extract for a citrusy taste. If you prefer almond or strawberry extract, you can use it—matter of fact, any extract that strikes your fancy.

FROSTED CHOCOLATE POUND CAKE

Milk chocolate frosting makes this classic recipe real festive. Since you bake it in a Bundt or tube pan, it makes a great birthday cake or dessert for after supper. Boxed cake mix might be easy, but after just one bite of this, you won't go back there ever again.

INGREDIENTS

cake

- 1 cup (2 sticks) unsalted butter, at room temperature, plus more for the pan
- 2½ cups all-purpose flour, plus more for the pan
- ⅛ teaspoon salt
- 1½ cups granulated sugar
- 4 large eggs
- 8 ounces milk chocolate, chopped and melted
- ½ cup chocolate syrup
- 2 teaspoons pure vanilla extract
- 1 cup well-shaken buttermilk (see Blue Ribbon Tip, page 22)
- 1 cup chopped toasted walnuts or pecans (optional)

frosting

- 4 cups confectioner's sugar, sifted, plus more for dusting
- Pinch of salt
- ½ cup (1 stick) unsalted butter, at room temperature
- ½ cup shortening (I use Crisco)
- 2 tablespoons whole milk, or more if needed
- 2 teaspoons pure vanilla extract
- 8 ounces milk chocolate, chopped and melted

DIRECTIONS

Preheat the oven to 325°F. Butter and flour a 10-inch Bundt or tube pan.

Make the cake: In a medium bowl, sift together the flour and salt. Using an electric mixer, beat the butter and granulated sugar until fluffy. Add the eggs, one at a time, blending well after each addition. Mix in the melted chocolate, chocolate syrup, and vanilla extract. Add the flour mixture alternating with the buttermilk. Use a rubber spatula to fold in the nuts, if using.

Pour the batter into the pan and bake until a cake tester or toothpick inserted into the center of the cake comes out dry, about 1 hour. Let cool in the pan on a wire rack for

15 minutes before turning out of the pan onto the rack to cool completely.

Whip the frosting: Using an electric mixer, combine the confectioner's sugar and salt. Add the butter, shortening, milk, and vanilla extract and beat until fluffy. Add the melted chocolate and beat until smooth. If the frosting is too thick, add milk by the teaspoon to improve the spreading consistency.

Spread the frosting over the top of the cooled cake and then dust with confectioner's sugar.

MAKES ONE 10-INCH BUNDT OF TUBE CAKE

 ELVIS CAKE Make a peanut butter frosting (see page 108) for this cake, top with sautéed bananas (cook them in a little butter until light golden brown), and you'll have a cake Elvis would have loved.

 BLUE RIBBON TIP To freeze this cake (and most others), do not frost, wrap the cake tightly in plastic wrap, and freeze for up to 1 month. Let the cake sit on the counter until defrosted, then whip up the frosting and spread it on top. The cake will be fresh as a daisy for a last-minute get-together!

BLUE RIBBON PUMPKIN CAKE

This is definitely *not* your average pumpkin cake, but it *is* one of the best I've got. I came up with this one playing around in the kitchen before a pumpkin cook-off, and, would you believe, it won that big old blue ribbon. It's different—with a whole lot of flavors and textures—but they're all balanced. In each slice, you get the chocolate from the Oreos on top, the crunch of the mixed nuts, and then the smoothness of the cake. The mixed party nuts sound a little bit crazy, but, I promise, they work—they give every bite just a bit of a distinct flavor from the last one. Greek yogurt makes a real rich batter, and the lemon-flavored kind is just so good with the pumpkin.

INGREDIENTS

cookie crunch

- 1 cup (2 sticks) unsalted butter, melted, plus more for the pans
- 1 (14-ounce) package Oreo cookies
- 1 (8- to 10-ounce) can salted mixed nuts
- 1 cup firmly packed light brown sugar

cake

- 1½ cups granulated sugar
- ¾ cup (1½ sticks) unsalted butter, at room temperature
- 3 cups pure pumpkin puree (about 1½ 15-ounce cans)
- 2¾ cups self-rising flour (I use White Lily)
- ½ cup lemon-flavored or plain Greek yogurt
- 1 tablespoon ground cinnamon
- 1 tablespoon pumpkin pie spice
- 1 tablespoon pure vanilla extract
- 4 large eggs

frosting

- 6 (8-ounce packages) cream cheese, at room temperature
- 1 cup (2 sticks) unsalted butter, at room temperature
- 3½ cups confectioner's sugar
- 2 tablespoons pure vanilla extract

chocolate topping

- ½ cup eggnog
- 1¼ cups chopped dark chocolate

recipe continues

Make the cookie crunch: Butter four 9-inch cake pans.

Using a food processor, pulse the Oreos until finely ground. Transfer to a medium bowl. Pulse the nuts until finely chopped. Add to the Oreo crumbs along with the brown sugar and mix well. Pour in the butter and mix until fully incorporated.

Divide the crunch topping mixture among the cake pans, pressing onto the bottom of each and spreading evenly.

Preheat the oven to 350°F.

Start the cake: Using an electric mixer, beat the granulated sugar and butter until light and fluffy, about 5 minutes, scraping down the sides of the bowl frequently. Add the pumpkin, flour, yogurt, cinnamon, pumpkin pie spice, and vanilla extract and mix until just blended. Add the eggs, one at a time, mixing well after each addition, and mix until just blended.

Divide the batter equally over the cookie crunch in each of the cake pans, smoothing the top of the batter evenly. Bake until a cake tester or toothpick inserted in the center of the cake comes out clean, 25 to 30 minutes. Remove from the oven and let cool completely in the pans on wire racks.

While the cakes are cooling, make the frosting: Using an electric mixer, whip the cream cheese and butter until very smooth and creamy. With the mixer on low speed, gradually add the confectioner's sugar and mix until smooth. Add the vanilla extract and mix well.

When the cakes are completely cool, unmold them. Frost the Oreo side (top) of each layer and then stack them, cake side down, to put the cake together. Spread the remaining frosting on the top and sides.

Refrigerate the cake or keep it in a cool place so that the frosting doesn't melt.

Before serving, prepare the chocolate topping: In a saucepan, bring the eggnog just to a simmer and then add the chocolate. Remove from the heat and stir until the chocolate has fully melted. Drizzle over the cake and let set before serving.

MaKes One 9-INCH Layer CaKe

Soda Pop Cake

I made this cake on *The American Baking Competition,* and everyone went nuts for it. But I was, like, *Have you people not* seen *Coca-Cola cake before?* That's just crazy! Around here, it's a classic, probably put out a hundred years ago by some cola company. Nana used to make it for me with Pepsi, which they call "the drink of the Carolinas," but I'm more of a Coca-Cola gal. (Even got a tattoo of a Coke bottle on me—with permission from the company itself!) You can make this cake with any kind of caramel-colored soda pop: Dr Pepper, Cheerwine, even Diet Coke. You'll be amazed what you can use soda pop for in baking—I even put 7UP in one of my biscuit recipes; it just makes them light and perfect.

INGREDIENTS ....

cake

- 1 cup (2 sticks) unsalted butter, plus more for the pan
- 2 cups self-rising flour (I use White Lily), plus more for the pan
- 2 cups granulated sugar
- 1 cup Coca-Cola
- 3 tablespoons unsweetened cocoa powder

- 1½ cups miniature marshmallows
- 2 large eggs, beaten
- ½ cup well-shaken buttermilk (see Blue Ribbon Tip, page 22)
- 1 teaspoon baking soda
- 1 teaspoon pure vanilla extract

frosting

- ½ cup (1 stick) unsalted butter
- 6 tablespoons Coca-Cola
- 1 tablespoon unsweetened cocoa powder
- 1 (1-pound) box confectioner's sugar
- ½ cup chopped pecans

DIRECTIONS ....

Preheat the oven to 350°F. Grease and flour a 9 × 13-inch pan.

Make the cake: In a large bowl, whisk together the flour and granulated sugar. In a saucepan, combine the Coca-Cola, cocoa powder, marshmallows, and butter. Bring to a boil, then remove from the heat, and whisk into the flour mixture.

In a separate bowl, whisk together the eggs, buttermilk, baking soda, and vanilla extract. Whisk into the cola mixture. Pour into the prepared pan and bake until a cake tester or toothpick inserted in the center of the cake comes out clean, about 35 minutes.

Make the frosting: In a saucepan, bring the butter, Coca-Cola, and cocoa powder to a boil over medium heat. Stir in the confectioner's sugar and mix well. Remove from the heat and stir in the pecans. Pour over the cake while both the cake and the frosting are still warm. Let cool before cutting into squares and serving.

MAKES ONE 9 × 13-INCH SHEET CAKE

 BLUE RIBBON TIP Make sure to use a dark caramel-colored soda. Clear sodas just will not work; they do not mix well with the cocoa powder. By just changing the kind of soda you use, you will have people thinking you spent all day over a hot stove to make something different. You don't have to tell them your secret!

FUDGE CAKE

For a chocoholic, this here's heaven on earth. It's just as rich as can be—like eating a big ol' piece of fudge. This is another one I got from Nana's notebook, probably passed around her Baptist church—maybe still being passed around today! Those tablespoons of coffee tie everything right together and bring out that real deep chocolate.

INGREDIENTS

cake
- ¾ cup (1½ sticks) unsalted butter, at room temperature, plus more for the pans
- 1¾ cups firmly packed light brown sugar
- 2 large eggs
- 1¼ cups well-shaken buttermilk (see Blue Ribbon Tip, page 22)
- 1 teaspoon pure vanilla extract
- 1 teaspoon pure almond extract

- 2 tablespoons strong black coffee, cooled
- 2 cups all-purpose flour
- ¾ cup unsweetened cocoa powder
- 1¼ teaspoons baking soda
- ½ teaspoon salt

frosting
- ½ cup (1 stick) unsalted butter or margarine, at room temperature

- 1 (8-ounce) package cream cheese, at room temperature
- ¼ cup unsweetened cocoa powder
- 1 (1-pound) box confectioner's sugar
- 2 tablespoons well-shaken buttermilk
- 1 teaspoon pure vanilla extract

chocolate ganache
- 1 cup heavy cream
- 1 cup semisweet chocolate chips

DIRECTIONS

Preheat the oven to 350°F. Grease two 9-inch cake pans.

Make the cake: Using an electric mixer, beat together the butter, brown sugar, eggs, buttermilk, vanilla and almond extracts, and coffee. Add the flour, cocoa, baking soda, and salt and mix well until the ingredients are just incorporated.

Pour into the prepared pans and bake until a cake tester or toothpick inserted in the center of the cake comes out clean, 22 to 24 minutes.

Let cool in the pans for 15 minutes

recipe continues

before turning out onto wire racks to cool completely.

Make the frosting: Using an electric mixer, combine the butter, cream cheese, and cocoa on low speed. Add the confectioner's sugar, gradually increase the speed to high, and mix until light and fluffy. Add the buttermilk and vanilla extract and mix until smooth.

Frost the tops of the 2 cakes, stack them, and then frost the sides with the remaining frosting.

Make the chocolate ganache: Combine the heavy cream and chocolate chips in a medium microwave-safe bowl. Heat in the microwave on high for 30 seconds, whisk, and repeat until the chocolate is completely melted and the mixture is smooth, about 2 minutes total. Let cool until no longer hot but still pourable, 5 to 10 minutes.

Pour the ganache over the cake, letting it drip down the sides.

MAKES ONE 9-INCH LAYER CAKE

 BLUE RIBBON TIPS The better the chocolate, the better the cake. I'm all for sticking to a budget but some things I will pay extra for. If you use imitation chocolate, that's what this cake is going to taste like. I find that the fake stuff has a waxy taste; believe me, I have been doing this long enough that I've tasted it all!

It's not often that I say this, but this particular recipe can be doubled. Make two cakes at one time, freeze one for a quick fix, and eat the other one now.

apple cake
with brown sugar sauce

When fall comes, we get real good apples here in the Carolinas, so I get to baking with them. We bake with the seasons down here—if it ain't in season, don't use it. (In the winter, sometimes I'll use frozen berries—ones I put up myself in the summer.) I use a mix of local apples and you should use whatever ones you've got available, especially anything firm like Granny Smith or Fuji—just stay away from soft apples like Red or Golden Delicious. The simple brown sugar sauce goes just perfect with the cake—and vanilla ice cream.

INGREDIENTS

cake

- 1 cup vegetable oil, plus more for the pan
- 2 cups granulated sugar
- 3 large eggs
- 2 teaspoons pure vanilla extract
- 3 cups self-rising flour (I use White Lily)
- 1 teaspoon salt
- 1 teaspoon baking soda
- 3 cups finely chopped peeled apples (about 6)
- 1 cup chopped pecans

sauce

- 1 cup firmly packed light brown sugar
- ¾ cup (1½ sticks) unsalted butter
- ¼ cup whole milk

DIRECTIONS

Preheat the oven to 350°F. Grease a 10-inch Bundt or tube pan.

Make the cake: In a large bowl, mix the oil, granulated sugar, eggs, and vanilla extract. In a separate bowl, sift together the flour, salt, and baking soda. Add the flour mixture to the egg mixture and stir until combined. Use a rubber spatula to fold in the apples and pecans.

Pour the batter into the pan and bake until golden brown and a cake tester or toothpick inserted in the center of the cake comes out clean, about 1 hour. Remove from the oven.

Prepare the sauce: In a medium saucepan, bring the brown sugar, butter, and milk to a gentle boil and then cook for 3 minutes over medium heat, stirring constantly. Pour over the hot cake in the pan. Let the cake cool completely before unmolding from the pan and onto a serving plate.

MAKES ONE 10-INCH BUNDT OR TUBE CAKE

mama's easter coconut cake

Mama made this every Easter, no matter what, and we waited all year for it. We call it white cake, because it's all white—inside and out. The frosting on this is soft and gooey, almost like marshmallow. It's helpful to have a candy thermometer when making the frosting.

INGREDIENTS ....

cake
- ½ cup (1 stick) unsalted butter or margarine, at room temperature, plus more for the pans
- 2½ cups all-purpose flour, plus more for the pans
- 1 tablespoon baking powder
- ½ teaspoon salt

- 5 large egg whites
- 1½ cups sugar
- 1 cup whole or 2% milk
- 1 teaspoon pure vanilla extract
- ¼ teaspoon coconut extract
- ⅔ cup sweetened shredded coconut

frosting
- 1 cup sugar
- 4 large egg whites
- ½ teaspoon cream of tartar
- Pinch of salt
- ½ teaspoon pure vanilla extract
- ¼ teaspoon coconut extract
- 1½ to 2 cups sweetened coconut flakes, as needed

DIRECTIONS ....

Preheat the oven to 350°F. Grease two 9-inch round cake pans, or one 9 × 13-inch pan.

Make the cake: Sift together the flour, baking powder, and salt. Using an electric mixer, beat the egg whites until soft peaks form. You'll need the mixer to beat the butter and sugar, so transfer the whites to a new bowl if you're using a stand mixer; there's no need to clean the bowl or beater(s), though. Use the electric mixer to beat together the butter and sugar until fluffy. Mix in the egg whites. Add the flour mixture and the milk and continue mixing just until no traces of flour are left. Using a rubber spatula, fold in the vanilla and coconut extracts along with the coconut. The batter will be thick. Divide between the prepared pans.

Bake until a cake tester or toothpick inserted in the center of the cake comes out clean, 25 to 30 minutes. It is important not to overcook this cake or it will be tough. If making a layer cake, let cool for 10 minutes in the pans before unmolding onto a wire rack. Let cool completely.

Make the frosting: Bring the sugar and ¼ cup water to a boil on top of the stove. Do not stir. Cook until the sugar reaches 238°F on a candy thermometer or the soft-ball stage (see Blue Ribbon Tip, page 193).

Meanwhile, using an electric mixer, whip the egg whites, cream of tartar, salt, vanilla extract, and coconut extract until stiff peaks form. When the sugar mixture reaches 238°F, remove it from the heat and carefully start pouring it into the egg white mixture while mixing on high speed.

Once all of the sugar has been added, whip until the frosting is spreading consistency, about 1 minute.

Spread the frosting on the first layer of cake, sprinkle with some of the coconut flakes, and add the top layer. Frost the top and sides; the frosting should be thick. Add the coconut flakes to the top and sides until the entire cake is covered with coconut. If making a sheet cake, simply frost the top and sprinkle with coconut.

MAKES ONE 9-INCH LAYER CAKE, OR ONE 9 × 13-INCH SHEET CAKE

 FRUIT COCKTAIL CAKE When Mama would bake this cake, sometimes she'd surprise us, and we wouldn't know if it was going to be fruit cocktail or regular coconut 'til she sliced into it. To make the fruity version, drain and add 1 (15-ounce) can of fruit cocktail to the mix.

Granny's Queen Cake

Every Thanksgiving, and only on Thanksgiving, Granny made us this cake. On that Thursday in November, we knew we'd be getting the world's best mac 'n' cheese and this cake, which is fit for a queen. It's like a Hummingbird Cake, but, back then, they didn't call it that. The bananas and pineapple go together real well, and I love the crunchy pecans and fall spices in it, too. This ain't no plain-Jane cake, I'll tell you that!

INGREDIENTS

cake
- 1½ cups vegetable oil, plus more for the pans
- 3 cups all-purpose flour
- 1½ cups granulated sugar
- 1 teaspoon baking soda
- 1 teaspoon salt
- 1½ teaspoons ground cinnamon
- ½ teaspoon ground nutmeg
- 3 large eggs
- 2 teaspoons pure vanilla extract
- 1 (8-ounce) can crushed pineapple, with juice
- 2 cups mashed bananas (about 3 large)
- 1½ cups chopped pecans

frosting
- 1 (8-ounce) package cream cheese, at room temperature
- ½ cup (1 stick) unsalted butter or margarine, at room temperature
- 3 cups confectioner's sugar
- 1 teaspoon pure vanilla extract
- ½ teaspoon pure almond extract
- 1 cup chopped pecans or black walnuts

DIRECTIONS

Preheat the oven to 350°F. Grease three 9-inch round cake pans, or a 9 × 13-inch pan.

Make the cake: Whisk together the flour, granulated sugar, baking soda, salt, cinnamon, and nutmeg. Add the eggs, oil, vanilla extract, pineapple with its juice, bananas, and pecans and mix with a spoon until combined. Pour the batter into the prepared pans and bake until a cake tester or toothpick inserted in the center of the cake comes out clean, 30 to 35 minutes. If making a layer cake, let cool in the pans for 5 minutes, before unmolding onto wire racks. Let cool completely.

Make the frosting: Using an electric mixer, whip the cream cheese, butter, confectioner's sugar, vanilla extract, and almond extract until smooth and of spreading consistency. Stir in the nuts. If the frosting is too thin, chill for a few minutes to stiffen.

Frost the tops of the 3 cakes, stack them, and then frost the sides with the remaining frosting, or simply frost the top if making a sheet cake.

MAKES ONE 9-INCH LAYER CAKE, OR ONE 9 × 13-INCH SHEET CAKE

 BLUE RIBBON TIP If I'm making this cake for home, I make it as a layer cake, but if I'm making it to take somewhere, I always make it in a 9 × 13-inch pan so I can get more slices out of it.

OLD-FASHIONED CARROT CAKE

My Nana used to make this with me, and my job was to grate the carrots—carrot after carrot after carrot on my little old box grater. Today, I make it the same way, and despite all the work, this is my number-one favorite cake. I'd rather it eat more than any other dessert—even more than chocolate, if you can believe it! Everybody knows someone who just loves carrot cake, and you got to please your friends and family, people—that's what this whole baking thang's about!

INGREDIENTS

- 1¼ cups vegetable oil, plus more for the pans
- 2½ cups all-purpose flour
- 2 teaspoons baking soda
- 2 teaspoons baking powder
- 2 teaspoons ground cinnamon
- ½ teaspoon salt
- 1½ cups sugar
- 4 large eggs
- 1 teaspoon pure vanilla extract
- 2 cups grated peeled carrots
- 1 cup chopped pecans (optional), plus more for sprinkling
- 1 cup raisins (optional)
- Cream Cheese Frosting (page 102)

DIRECTIONS

Preheat the oven to 350°F. Grease two 9-inch round cake pans, or a 9 × 13-inch pan.

In a large bowl, whisk together the flour, baking soda, baking powder, cinnamon, and salt. Using an electric mixer, beat the oil, sugar, eggs, and vanilla extract until creamy and pale yellow. Add the flour mixture and mix well. Add the carrots and continue mixing until just combined. If using the pecans and/or raisins, fold them in with a rubber spatula.

Pour the batter into the pans and bake until a cake tester or toothpick inserted in the center of the cake comes out clean, 35 to 40 minutes. If making a layer cake, let cool in the pans for 5 minutes, before unmolding onto wire racks. Let cool completely.

Frost the tops of the 2 cakes, stack them, and then frost the sides with the remaining frosting, or simply frost the top if making a sheet cake. Sprinkle with pecans, if desired.

MAKES ONE 9-INCH LAYER CAKE, OR ONE 9 × 13-INCH SHEET CAKE

CLASSIC PINEAPPLE CAKE

Most of the time, fresh fruit's just so much better than any canned thing you can buy. For baking, though, canned pineapple is real good. It's got that almost-citrus flavor to it, sour, sweet, and tropical-tasting; a little lemon extract in this cake helps, too. The glaze on top is just so easy to throw together and makes the cake fancier and even more lemon-flavored.

INGREDIENTS

cake
- 1 cup (2 sticks) unsalted butter, at room temperature, plus more for the pan
- 1½ cups granulated sugar
- 1 teaspoon ground cinnamon
- Pinch of salt

- 2 large eggs
- 2 large egg whites
- 1 teaspoon vanilla butter and nut flavoring
- 2 teaspoons lemon extract
- 2⅔ cups all-purpose flour
- 1 teaspoon baking powder

- 1 (16-ounce) can crushed pineapple, with juice

glaze
- 1 cup confectioner's sugar
- 1 tablespoon whole milk
- ½ teaspoon lemon extract

DIRECTIONS

Preheat the oven to 350°F. Grease a 10-inch Bundt or tube pan.

Make the cake: Using an electric mixer, beat the butter and granulated sugar until soft. Add the cinnamon, salt, eggs, and egg whites and mix until fully incorporated. Add the vanilla butter and nut flavoring and the lemon extract and beat until the mixture is fluffy.

In another bowl, whisk together the flour and baking powder. Gradually add the flour mixture to the egg mixture and mix until just combined. Mix in the pineapple with its juice.

Pour into the pan and bake until golden brown and a cake tester or toothpick inserted into the center of the cake comes out clean, 55 to 60 minutes. Let cool in the pan for 10 minutes, before turning out of the pan to cool completely on a wire rack.

While the cake is cooling, prepare the glaze: Sift the confectioner's sugar into a small bowl. Pour in the milk and lemon extract and mix until smooth. Drizzle over the cooled cake and let set before serving.

MAKES ONE 10-INCH BUNDT OR TUBE CAKE

cinnamon-chocolate cake

When I came up with the recipe for this cake, I was in major PMS mode—don't-talk-to-me, don't-mess-with-me, leave-me-alone-with-my-chocolate kinda thang. Cinnamon and chocolate work real well together and the yogurt makes the cake rich and satisfying without being too dang heavy. The frosting's easy to whip up, and the crunchy nut topping at the end gives some texture. I like to use pecans, but feel free to play around and use your favorite nut. Make this for a girlfriend if she's having a hard time, whether it's with the job, men, or kids; it'll sure brighten her mood.

INGREDIENTS

cake

- 1 cup (2 sticks) unsalted butter, plus more for the pans
- 2 cups self-rising flour (I use White Lily)
- 2 cups granulated sugar
- 1¼ teaspoons ground cinnamon
- ¼ cup unsweetened cocoa powder
- 2 large eggs
- ½ cup plain yogurt
- 1 teaspoon pure vanilla extract

frosting

- 1 (12-ounce) bag semisweet chocolate chips
- 4 tablespoons (½ stick) unsalted butter
- 3 tablespoons whole milk

topping

- ½ cup (1 stick) unsalted butter
- ⅓ cup whole milk
- 2 tablespoons unsweetened cocoa powder
- 1 cup confectioner's sugar
- 1 cup chopped pecans

DIRECTIONS

Preheat the oven to 350°F. Grease three 9-inch cake pans, or one 9 × 13-inch sheet pan.

Make the cake: Sift together the flour, granulated sugar, and cinnamon.

In a saucepan over medium heat, combine the butter, cocoa powder, and 1 cup water and stir until the butter mixture is melted and smooth. Remove from the heat.

In a bowl, whisk together the eggs, yogurt, and vanilla until smooth. Add the warm butter mixture and mix until fully blended. Add the flour mixture and beat until just combined.

Pour the batter into the pans. Bake until a cake tester or toothpick inserted in the center of the cake comes out clean, 22 to 25 minutes. If making a layer cake, let cool in the pans on wire racks for 10 minutes before unmolding onto wire racks. Let cool completely.

Make the frosting: Melt the chocolate chips, butter, and milk in a microwave or double boiler, stirring until smooth. Let cool until spreadable. Frost the tops of the 3 cakes, stack them, and then frost the sides with the remaining frosting, or simply frost the top if making a sheet cake.

Make the topping: In a saucepan over medium heat, bring the butter, milk, and cocoa powder to a boil. Stir in the confectioner's sugar and nuts. Let cool until warm, about 10 minutes, and then pour over the cake. Let set before serving.

MAKES ONE 9-INCH LAYER CAKE, OR ONE 9 × 13-INCH SHEET CAKE

keep-the-hubby-at-home cake

Here in Pickens, South Carolina, we're fishing people. One day, I was messing around with recipes for the Alabama peanut festival while my husband was getting ready for a carp-fishing competition. They usually set out in the afternoon and don't come back until 2 am or later, trying to catch as many of the big ol' goldfish as they can. I stuck the cake in the freezer to cool it down, and my husband, who caught a glimpse of it, asked what the heck I was making. When I described the recipe—a combination of chocolate, peanut butter, and just a hint of coffee—he said it sounded like one of the best things I ever made. He put his fishing rod down, took off his shoes, and decided to stick around for a bite of this cake. Not much can keep him from fishing, so I knew this one would be a hit.

INGREDIENTS

cake

- 1 cup vegetable oil, plus more for the pans
- 3½ cups self-rising flour (I use White Lily), plus more for the pans
- 2¼ cups granulated sugar
- 4 large eggs
- ¼ cup creamy peanut butter (I use Jif)
- 1½ teaspoons pure vanilla extract
- 1 cup well-shaken buttermilk (see Blue Ribbon Tip, page 22)
- 1½ cups coffee, at room temperature
- 1 cup unsweetened cocoa powder

frosting

- 1 (8-ounce) package cream cheese, at room temperature
- ¾ cup confectioner's sugar
- 1¼ cups creamy peanut butter (I use Jif)
- 1 cup chopped pecans (optional)
- 12 ounces frozen nondairy whipped topping, thawed
- 2½ cups chopped Reese's Peanut Butter Cups
- Chocolate syrup, for garnish

DIRECTIONS

Preheat the oven to 350°F. Grease and flour two 9-inch round pans.

Make the cake: Using an electric mixer, combine the oil, granulated sugar, eggs, peanut butter, and vanilla extract and beat until combined. Then mix in the buttermilk and coffee. Gradually add the flour and cocoa powder and beat for 2 to 3 minutes on medium speed.

Pour the batter into the prepared pans and bake until a cake tester or toothpick inserted in the center of the cake comes out clean, about 50 minutes. Let cool in the pans for 5 minutes before unmolding onto wire racks to cool completely.

Make the frosting: Using an electric mixer, mix the cream cheese, confectioner's sugar, and peanut butter until smooth. Then add the chopped pecans, if using. Using a rubber spatula, fold in the whipped topping until smooth. Refrigerate the frosting until stiff, about 1 hour.

Spread the frosting on the cooled cake layers, stack the layers, and frost the sides. Top with the chopped Reese's Peanut Butter Cups and drizzle with chocolate syrup.

MAKES ONE 9-INCH LAYER CAKE

 BLUE RIBBON TIP Don't worry if the batter seems liquidy when you put it in the oven. There's a good amount of liquid in there and the ingredients make for a melt-in-your-mouth texture in the final cake. The combination of whipped topping and sugar holds the frosting together perfectly, without making it too sweet. It's kind of like a peanut butter mousse, and it's so good, you'll want to eat it plain with a spoon.

mama's strawberry cake

Mama used to always make strawberry cake, so I named this one after her. It won the blue ribbon in the South Carolina state strawberry cook-off one May and then it took off. I had to make it for everyone in town!

INGREDIENTS ....

cake
- 4 tablespoons (½ stick) unsalted butter, at room temperature, plus more for the pans
- ½ cup granulated sugar
- 3 cups self-rising flour (I use White Lily)
- 4 large eggs
- ½ cup vegetable oil
- 1 (3¼-ounce) packet strawberry Jell-O
- 1 pint strawberries, crushed

topping
- 1 cup semisweet chocolate chips
- 2 tablespoons heavy cream

frosting and filling
- 1 (1-pound) box confectioner's sugar
- ½ cup (1 stick) unsalted butter, at room temperature
- ½ cup crushed strawberries
- 1 pint strawberries, sliced

- Whole strawberries, for garnish

DIRECTIONS ....

Preheat the oven to 350°F. Grease three 8-inch round cake pans.

Make the cake: Using an electric mixer, beat the butter and granulated sugar until fluffy. Add the flour, eggs, oil, ½ cup of water, and the Jell-O and mix until completely combined. Mix in the crushed strawberries. Divide the batter among the pans and bake until the tops are browned and a cake tester or toothpick inserted in the center of the cake comes out clean, about 30 minutes. Let cool in the pans for 5 minutes, before unmolding onto wire racks to cool completely.

Make the topping: Melt the chocolate chips with the cream in a microwave or double boiler, stirring until smooth. Set aside to cool slightly.

Whip the frosting: Using an electric mixer, whip the confectioner's sugar, butter, and crushed strawberries until smooth and a spreadable consistency.

Spread the frosting on top of each layer and top two of the layers with the sliced strawberries. Stack the layers, leaving the strawberry-free one for the top, frost the sides, and then pour the chocolate topping over the cake. Garnish with the whole strawberries.

Makes one 8-inch layer cake

orange creamsicle cake

Nana made me this cake for my birthday every year. I just love citrus so much—Key lime, lemon, anything like that—so, of course, I love orange, too. This cake has a whole lot of orange flavor from the zest and freshly squeezed juice. The cake itself is real light and fluffy and the filling's got that rich Creamsicle taste.

INGREDIENTS

2 oranges

cake
- 1 cup (2 sticks) unsalted butter, at room temperature, plus more for the pans
- 1 cup all-purpose flour, plus more for the pans
- 1 cup superfine sugar
- 4 large eggs
- 1 teaspoon vanilla paste (see Blue Ribbon Tip, opposite)
- 1 teaspoon baking powder

filling
- ½ cup (1 stick) plus 1 tablespoon unsalted butter, at room temperature
- 1 cup confectioner's sugar, sifted

icing
- 1⅓ cups confectioner's sugar, sifted

DIRECTIONS

Preheat the oven to 350°F. Grate the zest from the oranges and then juice the oranges. Keep the zest and juice separate.

Make the cake: Brush the sides of two 8-inch round cake pans with butter and dust with flour. Line the base of each pan with parchment paper and grease the paper.

Using an electric mixer, beat the butter until smooth. Gradually add the superfine sugar and half of the orange zest and beat until the mixture is light and fluffy. Add the eggs, one at a time, beating well after each addition. Mix in the vanilla paste. Sift together the flour and baking powder. Add the flour mixture to the egg mixture and mix until incorporated. Gently stir in 1 tablespoon of the orange juice.

Divide the batter evenly between the prepared pans and bake until a cake tester or toothpick inserted in the center comes out clean, 25 to 30 minutes. Let the cakes sit for 5 minutes in the pans before unmolding onto wire racks to cool completely.

Make the filling: Using an electric mixer, beat the butter until smooth, and then add the confectioner's sugar and the remaining orange zest. Gradually beat in 1 tablespoon of the orange juice to create a smooth, soft mixture. Spread evenly between the layers of the cooled cake.

Make the icing: Mix the confectioner's sugar with enough of the remaining orange juice to make a spreadable icing; you'll need about ¼ cup. If the icing is too soft, it will run off the cake, but if it is too stiff, it will be difficult to pour. Pour the icing on top of the cake, and let drip down the sides.

MAKES ONE 8-INCH LAYER CAKE

 BLUE RIBBON TIP Vanilla paste is ground vanilla beans and it is more economical than buying the whole beans, which are hard to find, to boot. It's stronger than vanilla extract and I use it when I want that extra vanilla-y flavor.

german cobbler cake

Growing up, we never got those fancy birthday cakes from the bakery with all the writing and stuff on them; we got homemade cakes because we were a family of bakers. This recipe was a real popular birthday cake, and we made it at Christmastime, too. It's like German chocolate cake, but a little bit different; I don't frost the sides and I drizzle chocolate over the top. Nana called this a "cobbler cake" and so I do, too, though I can't tell you why!

INGREDIENTS

cake

- 1 cup (2 sticks) unsalted butter, at room temperature, plus more for the pans
- 4 ounces German's sweet chocolate, chopped (I use Baker's)
- 4 large egg whites
- 2 cups sugar
- 4 large egg yolks
- 1½ teaspoons pure vanilla extract
- 2½ cups cake flour
- 1 teaspoon baking soda
- ½ teaspoon salt
- 1 teaspoon espresso powder
- 1 cup well-shaken buttermilk (see Blue Ribbon Tip, page 22)

frosting

- 1½ cups sugar
- 1 (12-ounce) can evaporated milk
- ¾ cup (1½ sticks) unsalted butter
- 5 large egg yolks, beaten
- 2 cups sweetened flaked coconut
- 1½ cups chopped pecans
- 1 teaspoon pure vanilla extract

chocolate drizzle

- 2 ounces semisweet chocolate, chopped, or chocolate chips
- 1 teaspoon shortening (I use Crisco)
- 2 teaspoons pure vanilla extract

DIRECTIONS

Preheat the oven to 350°F. Grease three 9-inch round baking pans, line with parchment paper, and grease the paper.

Make the cake: In small saucepan, melt the chocolate with ¼ cup of water over low heat, stirring until smooth. Set aside to cool.

Using an electric mixer, whip the egg whites until they hold stiff peaks. You'll need the mixer to beat the butter and sugar, so transfer the whites to a new bowl if you're using a stand mixer; there's no need to clean the bowl or beater(s), though.

Using the electric mixer, beat the butter and sugar until light and fluffy. One at a time, mix in the egg yolks, beating well after each addition. Blend in the melted chocolate and the vanilla extract. Sift together the flour, baking soda, salt, and espresso powder. Alternate adding the flour mixture and the buttermilk to the chocolate mixture, beating until combined. Using a rubber spatula, gently fold the egg whites into the batter.

Divide the batter among the prepared pans and bake until a cake tester or toothpick inserted in the center of the cake comes out clean, 22 to 24 minutes. Let cool for 10 minutes in the pans before unmolding onto wire racks to cool completely.

Make the frosting: In a small saucepan, heat the sugar, evaporated milk, butter, and egg yolks over medium-low heat, stirring constantly, until the mixture is thickened and golden brown, about 10 minutes. Make sure to stir constantly to prevent the eggs from curdling. Remove from the heat and stir in the coconut, pecans, and vanilla extract. Let cool until thick enough to spread.

Spread a third of the frosting over each cooled cake layer and stack the layers.

Make the chocolate drizzle: In a microwave or double boiler, melt the chocolate and shortening. Add the vanilla and stir until smooth. Drizzle over the cake and serve.

MAKES ONE 9-INCH LAYER CAKE

cheesecakes

chapter
4

"NEKKED" CHEESECAKE

PEANUT BUTTER CUP
CHEESECAKE

APPLE-CARAMEL CHEESECAKE

SALTED CARAMEL
CHEESECAKE

NO-BAKE OREO CHEESECAKE

BLACK BOTTOM CHEESECAKE

CAN'T-LIVE-WITHOUT-IT
PUMPKIN CHEESECAKE

WHITE CHOCOLATE-
PEPPERMINT CHEESECAKE

COCONUT-PECAN SWEET
POTATO CHEESECAKE

KEY LIME CHEESECAKE

TURTLE CHEESECAKE

EGGNOG CHEESECAKE

"NEKKED" CHEESECAKE

This is a plain-Jane, basic, New York–style cheesecake that I learned from Mama. Like a lot of people, she didn't like all the froufrou—wild and crazy toppings and all the rest of that—so this was her easy go-to recipe. The crust has a cakey, not crumbly, texture. If you're scared of making cheesecake, or just have a taste for the simple, this is your recipe.

Why's it called "nekked"? Well, we started pronouncing "naked" like that after a Ray Stevens song from the '70s. Somehow, like Mama always warned, it stuck.

INGREDIENTS

crust
- Nonstick cooking spray
- 1½ cups all-purpose flour
- ⅓ cup sugar
- ½ cup (1 stick) unsalted butter, at room temperature
- 1 large egg, beaten

filling
- 5 (8-ounce) packages cream cheese, at room temperature
- 1¾ cups sugar
- 5 large eggs
- 2 large egg yolks
- 3 tablespoons all-purpose flour
- ½ cup heavy cream

DIRECTIONS

Preheat the oven to 400°F. Lightly coat a 10-inch springform pan with cooking spray.

Make the crust: Using a fork, combine the flour, sugar, butter, and egg until the dough comes together. Press evenly onto the bottom and up the sides of the pan and then prick all over with a fork. Bake until very light brown, about 15 minutes. Remove from the oven and set aside to cool.

Increase the oven temperature to 475°F.

Prepare the filling: Using an electric mixer, combine the cream cheese, sugar, eggs, egg yolks, and flour. Add the cream and mix until just blended. Let the filling rest for about 5 minutes to allow air bubbles to rise to the surface.

Pour the filling into the crust and bake for 10 minutes. Decrease the oven temperature to 200°F and continue to bake the cheesecake for 1 hour.

Turn off the oven, but leave the cheesecake inside for an additional hour. It will be golden brown, but not completely firm.

Run a knife around the edges of the cake to loosen it from the pan and then let cool completely on a wire rack before removing the sides. Refrigerate overnight before serving.

MAKES ONE 10-INCH CHEESECAKE

 BLUE RIBBON TIP It's a fine balance between raw and overbaked when it comes to cheesecake. Keep in mind that each oven can vary in temperature, so watch closely as the cheesecake gets to the 60-minute mark. The top center part of the cheesecake (a 2- or 3-inch circle) should still be slightly soft and jiggly when you turn off the oven (or—for other cheesecake recipes in this book—when you take it out of the oven). It'll keep cooking a little and will set up once chilled.

Peanut Butter Cup Cheesecake

Now, this cheesecake brings me back to the good old days, when my husband, Mark, and I were first dating. I wanted to make him an extra special cake, and since peanut butter and cheesecake are two of his favorite things, I put them together and this is what he got. He loved it, and I have been making it ever since. The Nutter Butter crust and smooth peanut butter filling sure do scratch a peanut butter itch—and they just might get you a ring one day.

INGREDIENTS

crust
- 4 tablespoons (½ stick) unsalted butter, melted, plus more for the pan
- 18 Nutter Butter cookies, crushed

filling
- 4 (8-ounce) packages cream cheese, at room temperature
- 1 cup sugar
- ½ cup creamy peanut butter (I use Jif)
- ½ cup sour cream
- 1 teaspoon pure vanilla extract
- 3 large eggs

- 10 mini peanut butter cups, cut into quarters

topping
- ⅓ cup creamy peanut butter (I use Jif)
- ⅓ cup whole milk
- ½ cup semisweet chocolate chips
- 10 mini peanut butter cups, cut in half

DIRECTIONS

Preheat the oven to 300°F. Grease a 9-inch springform pan.

Make the crust: In a food processor, pulse the cookies until they are finely ground; you should have about 1½ cups. Add the butter and pulse again until well combined. Press onto the bottom and 1½ inches up the sides of the pan. Bake the crust until set, about 8 minutes. Set aside to cool.

Make the filling: Using an electric mixer, beat together the cream cheese, sugar, peanut butter, and sour cream until very smooth. Add the vanilla extract and then add the eggs, one at a time, mixing on low speed just until blended. Let the filling rest for about 5 minutes to allow air bubbles to rise to the surface.

Pour half of the batter into the crust and sprinkle half of the quartered peanut butter cups on top. Pour in the remaining batter and bake until the filling is set on the edges, but the middle still wiggles slightly when the pan is shaken gently, 45 to 55 minutes.

Sprinkle the remaining quartered peanut butter cups over the baked cheesecake. Run a knife around the edges of the cake to loosen it from the pan and then let cool completely on a wire rack before removing the sides.

Prepare the topping: Melt the peanut butter and drizzle over the cheesecake. Heat the milk until hot, either in a microwave or a double boiler, then add the chocolate chips, and let sit for 2 minutes. Stir until the chocolate is melted and smooth and then drizzle over the cheesecake. Top with the halved peanut butter cups and then refrigerate for at least 2 hours or overnight before serving.

MAKES ONE 9-INCH CHEESECAKE

apple-caramel cheesecake

I won a North Carolina State Apple Festival Grand Champion Ribbon with this one. If you like caramel apples, this is the cheesecake to go for. The Carolinas get some of the best apples in the country, and we stick to eating them in the fall, when they're in their prime. I use something firm here, like Granny Smith or Fuji. I usually use pecans, because I really like them with apples, but hazelnuts or black walnuts would be good in this, too. The caramel comes from all that butter and sugar, and it just cooks down and coats those apples something perfect. Serve this up when it's getting cold out, with a scoop of vanilla ice cream and a mug of hot apple cider in front of a warm fireplace.

INGREDIENTS

crust

- 1 cup graham cracker crumbs (about 14 crackers)
- ½ cup finely chopped pecans
- 3 tablespoons sugar
- ½ teaspoon ground cinnamon
- 4 tablespoons (½ stick) unsalted butter, melted

cheesecake filling

- 2 (8-ounce packages) cream cheese, at room temperature
- ½ cup sugar
- 2 large eggs
- ½ teaspoon pure vanilla extract

apple filling

- ⅓ cup sugar
- ½ teaspoon ground cinnamon
- 4 cups thinly sliced peeled apples
- ½ cup chopped pecans

DIRECTIONS

Preheat the oven to 350°F.

Make the crust: In a large bowl, stir together the graham cracker crumbs, pecans, sugar, cinnamon, and butter.

Press onto the bottom and a little bit up the sides of a 9-inch springform pan. Bake until set, about 10 minutes. Set aside on a wire rack to cool.

recipe continues

Prepare the cheesecake filling: Using an electric mixer, mix the cream cheese and sugar on medium speed. Beat in the eggs, one at a time, mixing well after each addition. Blend in the vanilla. Let the filling rest for about 5 minutes to allow air bubbles to rise to the surface. Pour the filling into the baked crust.

Prepare the apple filling: In a bowl, stir together the sugar and cinnamon. Toss with the apples to coat. Spoon the apple mixture over the cream cheese layer and sprinkle with the pecans. Bake until set and slightly browned on top, 60 to 70 minutes.

Run a knife around the edges of the cake to loosen it from the pan and then let cool completely on a wire rack before removing the sides. Refrigerate for at least 4 hours or overnight before serving.

MAKES ONE 9-INCH CHEESECAKE

salted caramel cheesecake

I know salted caramel and salted chocolates are all the rage now, but I've been making this cheesecake for years, before the craze, because they are real good eating together. This cheesecake's impressive, too—good for when the boss is coming to dinner, or any time you need a fancy-type dessert. There sure are a few steps on this one, but perfection doesn't ever come easy!

INGREDIENTS ....

crust
- 7 tablespoons salted butter, melted, plus more for the pan
- 1 (1-pound 10-ounce) family-sized package Oreo cookies

filling
- 3 (8-ounce) packages cream cheese, at room temperature
- 1 cup firmly packed light brown sugar
- 3 large eggs
- ¾ cup heavy cream

- ¼ cup caramel-flavored coffee syrup (see Blue Ribbon Tips, page 127)
- 1 teaspoon pure vanilla extract

caramel sauce
- ½ cup (1 stick) unsalted butter
- 1¼ cups firmly packed light brown sugar
- 2 tablespoons caramel-flavored coffee syrup (see Blue Ribbon Tips, page 127)
- ½ cup heavy cream

chocolate ganache
- 1 cup heavy cream
- 1 cup semisweet chocolate chips

stabilized whipped cream
- 1 teaspoon unflavored powdered gelatin
- 1½ cups heavy cream
- 2 tablespoons granulated sugar

- 1½ teaspoons flaky sea salt, such as Maldon

DIRECTIONS ....

Preheat the oven to 300°F. Grease a 9-inch springform pan.

Make the crust: Crush the Oreos to fine crumbs in a food processor. Add the butter and pulse until all of the crumbs are moistened. Press the mixture into the bottom and 1 inch up the sides of the pan. Put the pan in the freezer while preparing the filling.

recipe continues

Prepare the filling: Using an electric mixer, beat the cream cheese and brown sugar on medium speed until smooth. Beat in the eggs, one at a time, just until blended. Mix in the cream, coffee syrup, and vanilla extract. Let the filling rest for about 5 minutes to allow air bubbles to rise to the surface.

Pour the filling into the crust and bake until the edges of the cheesecake are set, but the center jiggles slightly, 1 hour and 10 minutes to 1 hour and 20 minutes.

Turn off the oven and open the door 4 inches. Let the cheesecake sit in the oven for 30 minutes. Run a thin knife around the edges of the pan to loosen the cheesecake, but do not remove the sides. Let cool on a wire rack for 30 minutes and then refrigerate for at least 6 hours or overnight.

Cook the caramel sauce: In a medium saucepan, melt the butter over medium heat. Add the brown sugar and coffee syrup and bring to a boil. Cook, stirring, until the sugar dissolves, about 1 minute. Stir in the cream and return to a boil. Remove from the heat, and let cool for 20 minutes, but do not let the mixture harden.

Remove the cheesecake from the refrigerator and pour the caramel sauce on top, using as much as you want and saving the rest to use for serving (or as a topping for ice cream). Return the cheesecake to the fridge.

Make the chocolate ganache: Combine the heavy cream and chocolate chips in a medium microwave-safe bowl. Heat in the microwave on high for 30 seconds, whisk, and repeat until the chocolate is completely melted and the mixture is smooth, about 2 minutes total. Let cool until no longer hot, but still pourable, 5 to 10 minutes.

Remove the cheesecake from the refrigerator and pour the ganache on top of the caramel layer. Return to the fridge.

Make the whipped cream: Pour ¼ cup cold water into a microwave-safe bowl or small saucepan and sprinkle the gelatin on top. Let the gelatin soften and absorb the water, about 5 minutes. Gently heat the gelatin and stir until it dissolves. Let cool until just warm.

Meanwhile, using an electric mixer, whip the cream and granulated sugar until soft peaks form. Slowly pour in the gelatin and mix until soft peaks form again.

Remove the cheesecake from the refrigerator, and using a pastry bag fitted with a small star tip, or a plastic bag with the corner cut off, pipe the whipped cream on the edges of the cake. Drizzle the top of the cake with caramel sauce and sprinkle with the sea salt. Cover and store in the refrigerator until ready to serve, or for up to 8 hours.

Before serving, run a thin knife around the edges of the pan before carefully removing the sides of the pan. Serve with additional caramel sauce, if desired.

MAKES ONE 9-INCH CHEESECAKE

 BLUE RIBBON TIPS I use Watkins brand caramel-flavored coffee syrup. If you can't find this flavor syrup, substitute plain caramel flavor mixed with ½ teaspoon espresso powder.

This whipped cream is good for lots of other desserts—the gelatin stabilizes it so it won't get all temperamental and weepy on you.

No-Bake Oreo Cheesecake

When I was pregnant with my daughter, a friend of mine made this for my baby shower, and I just knew I had to get that recipe. I'm still using it, twenty years later. Even though there's a bunch of steps, it's actually real easy and real rich. You can use any ready-made fudge sauce on this; I like a dark chocolate one made by Hershey's. You'll need 2 packages of Oreos for this recipe—they're everywhere!

INGREDIENTS

crust
- 5 tablespoons unsalted butter, melted, plus more for the pan
- 2½ cups Oreo cookie crumbs

filling
- 2¼ cups heavy cream
- 2 (8-ounce) packages cream cheese, at room temperature
- ⅔ cup sugar
- ½ teaspoon salt
- 2 teaspoons vanilla paste (see Blue Ribbon Tip, page 113)
- 1 tablespoon lemon juice
- 2½ cups Oreo cookie chunks, plus more for garnish
- ½ cup hot fudge sauce, at room temperature

DIRECTIONS

Make the crust: Grease a 9-inch springform pan.

Stir together the cookie crumbs and butter in a small bowl until the crumbs resemble wet grains of sand. Press the mixture onto the bottom of the pan; if you have extra crumb crust, you can go up the sides a little, as well.

Prepare the filling: Using an electric mixer, beat the heavy cream until medium peaks form.

Using an electric mixer, beat the cream cheese until smooth. Add the sugar, salt, vanilla paste, and lemon juice and beat until incorporated. Do not overmix.

Use a rubber spatula to fold the whipped cream into the cream cheese mixture. Fold the Oreo cookie chunks into the cream cheese mixture. Pour half of the filling into the crust and then pour the fudge sauce on top, spreading it with a butter knife. Do not overspread the fudge, or it will begin to blend with the cheesecake mixture. Pour the remaining cream cheese mixture over the fudge and smooth the top. Refrigerate for at least 6 hours or overnight.

Before serving, garnish the top with Oreo cookie chunks.

MAKES ONE 9-INCH CHEESECAKE

 BLUE RIBBON TIP One of the things I love about baking is that it leaves a lot to your own imagination. You can use any flavor of Oreo on the market to make this crust (trust me—I have!) and then spike the filling to match or swap the fudge topping for something else. The one thing I have found, though, is that store-bought cookies work better than homemade, which can get soggy. But in terms of places you can take this cheesecake, the sky is the limit. Reach for the stars!

Black Bottom Cheesecake

This one is for the brownie and cheesecake fans: a simple naked cheesecake on top with a rich, cakey, chocolaty bottom. I use Greek yogurt here because it's thick and substantial, and gives the cheesecake a sturdy texture. It also makes this a little less sweet, so it's not overbearing. If you want to put whipped topping on this, go ahead, but, personally, I think it's good just like it is.

INGREDIENTS

brownie layer
- ½ cup (1 stick) unsalted butter, at room temperature, plus more for the pan
- 1 cup all-purpose flour, plus more for the pan
- 4 ounces bittersweet chocolate, chopped
- 1 cup sugar
- 2 large eggs
- ¼ cup whole milk

cheesecake layer
- 5 (8-ounce) packages cream cheese, at room temperature
- ½ cup plain Greek yogurt
- ⅔ cup sugar
- 3 large eggs
- 1 teaspoon pure vanilla extract

DIRECTIONS

Preheat the oven to 350°F. Lightly grease and flour a 9-inch springform pan.

Make the brownie layer: Melt the butter and chocolate in a microwave or saucepan over low heat, stirring frequently until smooth. Remove from the heat.

Using an electric mixer, beat the sugar into the chocolate mixture and mix for 5 minutes. It will thicken as you mix.

Add the eggs and milk to the chocolate mixture and beat on medium speed. Mix in the flour until just blended. Spoon into the prepared pan and bake until set, about 25 minutes. Remove from the oven.

Decrease the oven temperature to 325°F.

Prepare the cheesecake layer: Using an electric mixer, beat together the cream cheese, yogurt, sugar, eggs, and vanilla, making sure there are no lumps. Let the filling rest for about 5 minutes to allow air bubbles to rise to the surface.

Pour the cream cheese mixture over the brownie base and bake until the center is almost set and the sides are very lightly browned, 50 to 55 minutes. Run a knife around the edges of the cake to loosen it from the pan and then let cool completely on a wire rack before removing the sides. Refrigerate for at least 4 hours or overnight before serving.

MAKES ONE 9-INCH CHEESECAKE

 BLACK BOTTOM CHEESECAKE WITH STRAWBERRY GLAZE When strawberries are in season, I like to use them to make a glaze for the top of this cheesecake: In a small saucepan, combine 1 pint strawberries, hulled and sliced, with ⅓ cup water, 2 tablespoons sugar, and 1½ teaspoons cornstarch. Cook over medium heat, stirring, until the mixture boils. Continue cooking and stirring until thickened and the juices are clear. Pour the strawberry mixture over the chilled cheesecake and let set before serving.

CAN'T-LIVE-WITHOUT-IT PUMPKIN CHEESECAKE

This is my stepson Jody's ultimate favorite dessert, and I make it for him whenever he begs enough for it. It's also a real good Thanksgiving dessert—different from the usual pumpkin and sweet potato pies. The gingersnap cookie crust has a whole lot of oomph and balances the pumpkin real nice.

INGREDIENTS

crust

- 3 tablespoons unsalted butter, melted, plus more for the pan
- 1½ cups gingersnap cookie crumbs (about 30 cookies)
- ¼ cup granulated sugar

filling

- 3 (8-ounce) packages cream cheese, at room temperature
- 1 cup granulated sugar
- ¼ cup firmly packed light brown sugar
- 2 large eggs
- 1 (15-ounce) can pure pumpkin puree
- ⅔ cup evaporated milk
- 2 tablespoons cornstarch
- 1 teaspoon ground cinnamon
- 1 teaspoon ground nutmeg
- ½ teaspoon ground ginger
- ½ teaspoon ground cloves

topping

- 1 (16-ounce) container sour cream
- ½ cup granulated sugar
- 1 teaspoon pumpkin spice mix
- 1 teaspoon pure vanilla extract

Broken gingersnap cookies, for garnish

DIRECTIONS

Preheat the oven to 350°F. Grease a 9-inch springform pan.

Make the crust: In a medium bowl, combine the cookie crumbs, butter, and granulated sugar and mix well. Press into the pan. Bake until set and firm, 6 to 8 minutes. Let cool on a wire rack for 10 minutes.

Prepare the filling: Using an electric mixer, beat the cream cheese, granulated sugar, and brown sugar until fluffy. Beat in the eggs, pumpkin, and evaporated milk. Add the cornstarch, cinnamon, nutmeg, ginger, and cloves and beat well. Let the filling rest for about 5 minutes to allow air bubbles to rise to the surface.

Pour the filling into the crust and bake until the edges are set and very lightly browned, but the center jiggles slightly, 65 to 75 minutes. Let cool completely on a wire rack.

Make the topping: Mix together the sour cream, granulated sugar, pumpkin spice mix, and vanilla extract in a small bowl. Spread over the cooled cheesecake and then refrigerate overnight.

Before serving, garnish with broken ginger snaps. Run a knife around the edges of the cake to loosen, remove the sides of the pan, and serve.

MAKES ONE 9-INCH CHEESECAKE

 BLUE RIBBON TIP Don't use those cans of pumpkin pie mix you see in stores. For one thing, the puree is loaded with spices, and two, it's very thin, which adds to the baking time and can result in a burned crust. I always use solid pumpkin, which is often labeled "pure pumpkin puree." It has no flavorings so you can add only the ones you like. If you don't like cloves, for example, why buy something that already has them mixed in? You can leave the cloves out of this recipe, if you prefer. Stick to your flavor guns, bakers, and say no to predetermined seasonings!

WHITE CHOCOLATE-PEPPERMINT CHEESECAKE

This here's one of the best Christmastime desserts you're ever going to find. I don't splurge on most anything, but when it comes to white chocolate, I go for the best, usually Ghirardelli. I just think the flavor is better. I like making this with a vanilla wafer crust, but it's also real good with an Oreo or chocolate cookie crust.

INGREDIENTS ....

crust
- 4 tablespoons (½ stick) unsalted butter, melted, plus more for the pan
- 2½ cups crushed vanilla wafers
- 4 ounces white chocolate

cheesecake
- 4 ounces white chocolate
- 3 (8-ounce) packages cream cheese, at room temperature
- 1½ cups sugar
- 6 large eggs

- 1 (16-ounce) container sour cream
- 25 starlight peppermint candies

DIRECTIONS ....

Preheat the oven to 350°F. Grease a 9-inch springform pan.

Make the crust: Mix together the vanilla wafers with the butter until all the crumbs are coated with butter. Press onto the bottom and halfway up the sides of the pan. Bake in the oven until set, about 20 minutes.

Meanwhile, melt the white chocolate in a microwave or double boiler. When the crust comes out of the oven, pour the white chocolate into the crust and smooth it out so that it covers the entire bottom. Chill in the refrigerator to harden, about 20 minutes.

Decrease the oven temperature to 300°F. Put a baking pan half filled with hot water on the bottom rack of the oven.

While the crust chills, prepare the cheesecake filling: Melt the white chocolate in a microwave or double boiler and set aside to cool slightly. Using an electric mixer, beat together the cream cheese and sugar. Add the eggs, one at a time, mixing until smooth after each addition. Mix in the sour cream and cooled melted chocolate.

Smash the mints into a fine powder using a rolling pin or a food processor and fold into the cheesecake mixture. Let the filling rest for about 5 minutes to allow air bubbles to rise to the surface.

Put the crust on a baking sheet and then pour in the cheesecake mixture, filling the crust to within ½ inch from the top.

Bake for 1 hour 30 minutes. Turn off the oven and let the cheesecake sit for 4 hours inside the oven.

Remove from the oven and refrigerate overnight.

When you are ready to serve, run a knife around the edges of the cake to loosen and then remove the sides of the pan. You can smooth the sides of the cheesecake with a damp butter knife if needed.

MAKES ONE 9-INCH CHEESECAKE

COCONUT-PECAN SWEET POTATO CHEESECAKE

This here's a real substantial dessert, not light or dainty or nothing. The flavors of the sweet potatoes, pecans, and coconut all work so good together, without the cheesecake being over-flavored. It's good during cooler weather, like fall, wintertime, or even early spring—when you're looking for something that's going to just fill you right on up. It's a real festive cheesecake, good for in-laws and family or a different Thanksgiving dessert.

This way of cooking your sweet taters works for regular taters, too. Steaming them in the microwave is fast and easy so you don't have to wait for those dang spuds to cook.

INGREDIENTS

crust

- 4 tablespoons (½ stick) unsalted butter, melted, plus more for the pan
- 2 cups graham cracker crumbs (about 28 crackers)
- 1 tablespoon light brown sugar
- 1 tablespoon granulated sugar

sweet potato filling

- 2 large sweet potatoes
- 2 tablespoons ground cinnamon
- 1 teaspoon ground allspice
- 1 teaspoon ground nutmeg
- ½ teaspoon ground ginger
- ½ cup heavy cream

cheesecake filling

- 2 (8-ounce) packages cream cheese, at room temperature
- 1½ cups granulated sugar
- Pinch of salt
- 4 large eggs
- ½ cup sour cream
- ⅓ cup all-purpose flour
- 2 tablespoons ground cinnamon
- 1 teaspoon pure vanilla extract

candied pecans

- 1 cup pecans
- 4 tablespoons (½ stick) unsalted butter, melted
- 2 tablespoons granulated sugar

topping

- ½ cup unsweetened shredded coconut
- ⅓ cup granulated sugar
- ½ teaspoon ground cinnamon

....

Preheat the oven to 350°F. Grease a 9-inch springform pan. Wrap the bottom and sides of the pan in a double layer of heavy-duty aluminum foil to prevent water from seeping into the cake during baking.

Make the crust: Mix together the graham cracker crumbs, butter, and both sugars. Firmly press the mixture onto the bottom and 1 inch up the sides of the prepared pan. Bake until set, 8 to 10 minutes. Remove to a wire rack to cool.

Increase the oven temperature to 450°F.

Meanwhile, make the sweet potato filling: Rinse the sweet potatoes and put them in a large plastic bag, leaving them wet. Microwave until they are very soft when poked with a fork, about 10 minutes. Scrape the flesh into a bowl and mix in the cinnamon, allspice, nutmeg, and ginger. Stir in the heavy cream.

Make the cheesecake filling: Using an electric mixer, beat the cream cheese until smooth. Add the granulated sugar, salt, and eggs, one at a time, mixing well after each addition. Mix in the sour cream, flour, cinnamon, and vanilla until combined. Gently fold in the sweet potato filling. Let the filling rest for about 5 minutes to allow air bubbles to rise to the surface.

Heat water until boiling in a saucepan or microwave. Put the cheesecake pan in a large roasting pan and carefully pour hot water into the roasting pan so that it comes halfway up the sides of the pan. Pour the filling into the crust. Bake for 15 minutes. Decrease the oven temperature to 250°F and bake until the center is just firm, an additional 45 minutes. Turn off the oven and let the cake cool in the oven for 30 minutes. Remove to a wire rack and let cool completely.

Make the candied pecans: In a microwave-safe bowl, combine the pecans, butter, and granulated sugar and microwave for 30 seconds. Mix well and set aside to cool.

Prepare the topping: Scatter the coconut in a skillet and set over medium heat. Sprinkle the granulated sugar on top and toast, shaking the pan, until the coconut is light brown, 8 to 10 minutes. Stir in the cinnamon and set aside to cool on a plate.

Scatter the pecans and coconut on top of the cooled cheesecake. Refrigerate for at least 2 hours before removing the sides of the pan and serving.

MAKES ONE 9-INCH CHEESECAKE

key Lime cheesecake

Since Key lime is my ultimate favorite pie and you can tell by the fact that I've got a whole chapter devoted to cheesecakes how much I like *them*, you can bet I've got a real good Key lime cheesecake for y'all. From half growing up in Florida (we moved there when I was eleven), this is a real staple in my life. I used to make it for the Fourth of July and my Daddy's birthday. His real birthday was July 3rd, but we celebrated him *and* the country on the 4th. This is one of those summer desserts you make when it's hot and you need something cool and refreshing—like for a big Fourth of July barbecue.

INGREDIENTS

crust
- ½ cup (1 stick) unsalted butter, melted, plus more for the pan
- 2 cups graham cracker crumbs (about 28 crackers)
- ¼ cup sugar

filling
- 6 large egg whites
- 3 (8-ounce) packages cream cheese, at room temperature
- 1¼ cups sugar
- 6 large egg yolks
- 1 (8-ounce) container sour cream
- 1½ teaspoons grated Key lime zest
- ½ cup fresh Key lime juice

DIRECTIONS

Preheat the oven to 350°F. Grease a 9-inch springform pan.

Make the crust: Mix together the graham cracker crumbs, sugar, and butter. Firmly press the mixture onto the bottom and 1 inch up the sides of the pan. Bake until set, about 8 minutes. Let cool on a wire rack. Leave the oven on.

Prepare the filling: Using an electric mixer, beat the egg whites until they hold stiff peaks. You'll need the mixer to beat the cream cheese, so transfer the whites to a new bowl if you're using a stand mixer; there's no need to clean the bowl or beater(s), though. Using the mixer, beat the cream cheese until creamy. Gradually beat in the sugar. Add the egg yolks, one at a time, beating well after each addition. Stir in the sour cream, lime zest, and lime juice. Let the filling rest for about 5 minutes to allow air bubbles to rise to the surface.

Gently fold the egg whites into the cream cheese mixture. Pour the batter into the crust and bake for 65 minutes. Turn off the oven, partially open the oven door, and let the cheesecake cool in the oven for 15 minutes. Remove from the oven and run a knife around the edges of the pan to release the sides. Let cool completely on a wire rack before removing the sides. Cover and refrigerate for at least 8 hours or overnight before serving.

Makes One 9-Inch Cheesecake

 Blue Ribbon Tip Key limes mean summer to me, and you can mix them with lots of summery flavors. Try topping this cheesecake with fresh strawberries or a strawberry glaze (see page 131), raspberries or a raspberry glaze, or mango slices and whipped cream. The key is balance. Always pair the tart with the sweet. Since the cheesecake is so tart, a sweet fruit topping works great.

TURTLE CHEESECAKE

With this recipe here, you get that caramel, creamy, chocolaty nuttiness without all that chewing fuss. This one doesn't have a specific time of year, so you don't have to wait for a holiday to make it. Try it on a Thursday night after your meatloaf supper and see what everyone says. Lemon juice might seem just a little bit strange in the filling, but it cuts the sweetness from the condensed milk and enhances the cream cheese with a citrus kick. I give a range for the chocolate chips and the caramel topping because some people like more of one or the other in their turtles. Play around, people, and find your flavor!

INGREDIENTS

crust

6 tablespoons (¾ stick) unsalted butter, melted, plus more for the pan

1½ cups graham cracker crumbs (about 21 crackers)

1½ tablespoons sugar

½ cup finely chopped walnuts or pecans

filling

2 (8-ounce) packages cream cheese, at room temperature

1 (14-ounce) can sweetened condensed milk

¼ cup fresh lemon juice

3 large eggs

½ to ¾ cup chocolate chips, to taste

⅓ cup caramel topping, or to taste

½ cup chopped walnuts or pecans

DIRECTIONS

Preheat the oven to 300°F. Grease a 9-inch springform pan.

Make the crust: Mix together the cracker crumbs, sugar, walnuts, and butter. Press onto the bottom and a little bit up the sides of the pan.

Prepare the filling: Using an electric mixer, blend the cream cheese until smooth. Mix in the condensed milk and lemon juice. Add the eggs, one at a time, mixing well after each addition. Let the filling rest for about 5 minutes to allow air bubbles to rise to the surface.

Pour the filling into the crust, then sprinkle the chocolate chips on top, and allow them to sink in. Bake until browned around the edges, but the center still jiggles slightly, 50 to 55 minutes.

Remove the cheesecake from the oven. Drizzle the caramel over the top and then sprinkle the nuts over it. Bake for an additional 5 minutes; the topping will resemble turtle candy.

Remove from the oven and let cool completely on a wire rack. Refrigerate for at least 4 hours before serving.

MAKES ONE 9-INCH CHEESECAKE

 BLUE RIBBON TIP Do not overbeat cheesecake batter. Blend the ingredients quickly, so you don't make too many air bubbles. If you get too many air pockets, they can make the cheesecake puff up too much while baking—and then crack when it cools.

eggnog cheesecake

We love our eggnog, me and the family, and when we find it in stores, we use it for every kind of baked good you can possibly think of. Eggnog cheesecake's real popular around Christmastime, for functions at church or with family, and this recipe's full of eggnog flavor, from the filling to the topping. The gingersnap crust just brings out that eggnog taste even more and makes it extra Christmas-like. Now I'm not a big drinker, but I imagine this would be good with a snifter of something by the fireplace—keep you warm inside and out.

INGREDIENTS

crust

- 4 tablespoons (½ stick) unsalted butter, melted, plus more for the pan
- 2½ cups gingersnap cookie crumbs (about 48 cookies)
- ¼ cup granulated sugar
- ½ teaspoon vanilla paste (see Blue Ribbon Tip, page 113)

filling

- 2 cups confectioner's sugar
- 2 tablespoons all-purpose flour
- 4 (8-ounce) packages cream cheese, at room temperature
- 1½ cups eggnog
- 4 large eggs, lightly beaten, at room temperature

topping

- 1 cup heavy cream
- ¼ cup confectioner's sugar
- ¼ cup eggnog

DIRECTIONS

Preheat the oven to 325°F. Grease a 10-inch round springform pan. Wrap the bottom and sides of the pan in a double layer of heavy-duty aluminum foil to prevent water from seeping into the cake during baking.

Make the crust: Mix together the gingersnap crumbs, granulated sugar, vanilla paste, and butter. Press firmly onto the bottom and about ½ inch up the sides of the prepared pan.

Prepare the filling: In a medium bowl, whisk together the confectioner's sugar and flour. Using an electric mixer, blend the cream cheese on medium speed until smooth. Add the confectioner's sugar mixture and then the eggnog, beating on medium-low speed after each ingredient until thoroughly combined. Add half of the eggs, beating until just combined. Scrape the bowl and add the remaining eggs, mixing until just combined. Let the filling rest for about 5 minutes to allow air bubbles to rise to the surface.

Heat water until boiling in a microwave or saucepan. Put the cheesecake pan in a large roasting pan and carefully pour enough hot water into the roasting pan so that it comes halfway up the sides of the pan. Pour the filling into the crust. Bake until the edges are set, but the center still jiggles, 1 hour 10 minutes to 1 hour 20 minutes. The cake should be slightly puffed up and just beginning to brown.

Remove the cheesecake from the oven and run a thin knife around the edges of the pan to loosen. Let cool completely on a wire rack. Cover and refrigerate for at least 12 hours or up to 24 hours.

Before serving, prepare the topping: Using an electric mixer, beat the cream until soft mounds form. Gradually add the confectioner's sugar and continue beating until thick and stiff. Slowly drizzle in the eggnog, continuing to beat until combined. Spread the topping evenly over the top of the chilled cheesecake, swirling decoratively.

MAKES ONE 10-INCH CHEESECAKE

SUNDAY GO-TO-MEETING

classic easy Banana PUDInG

Everybody thinks their grandma makes banana pudding better than anybody else's grandma; I think my mother-in-law makes the absolute best one in the world. This recipe is pretty basic and hard to screw up. There are variations if you're looking for them—some people use cream cheese instead of sour cream, for example—but the truth is, I like it the way it is. Halve this recipe if you want, though no one is ever going to be upset about leftovers, which just seem to get better in the fridge.

INGREDIENTS

- 2 large (5.1-ounce) boxes vanilla or banana cream instant pudding mix (or one of each, if you like)
- 1 quart whole milk
- 1 cup evaporated milk
- 1 (8-ounce container) sour cream
- 2 cups frozen nondairy whipped topping, thawed
- 1 (1-pound) bag vanilla wafers
- 4 or 5 large bananas, sliced

DIRECTIONS

In a large bowl, whisk together the pudding mix, whole milk, and evaporated milk until thickened. Using a rubber spatula, fold in the sour cream and 1 cup of the whipped topping. Refrigerate for 10 minutes.

Make a layer of vanilla wafers in the bottom of a 9 × 13-inch baking dish, arranging them with the flat side up (this will allow the mixture to better soak into the wafers). Scatter some of the banana slices over the wafers and then spoon some of the chilled pudding mixture on top, making sure to cover the fruit well. Repeat with another layer of wafers, bananas, and pudding and continue assembling until you run out of ingredients. Top with the remaining 1 cup whipped topping and stick wafers decoratively around the edges if you have some left over.

Refrigerate for at least 1 hour, although overnight is preferable.

serves 12 TO 15

peach cobbler

I usually stick to baking with fruits that are in season, but for cobblers, it's best to use fruit in syrup or in a juice. Sure, you can use fresh fruit, but you have to cook it down, so the fruit releases all that sugar, and, well, sometimes I just ain't got time for that. You can make this with anything in syrup you can find—apple pie filling or cherry filling works real well, even pineapple or mixed fruit cocktail. For once, if you're wanting peach cobbler in winter, you can just go ahead and whip it up, if you like. When this bakes, the batter rises up and makes an amazing crust.

INGREDIENTS

½ cup (1 stick)
   unsalted butter

¾ cup self-rising flour
   (I use White Lily)

1 cup sugar

¾ cup whole milk

1 (28-ounce) can
   peaches in heavy
   syrup, with juice

1 teaspoon ground
   cinnamon (optional)

DIRECTIONS

Preheat the oven to 350°F. While the oven is heating, put the butter in a 9 × 13-inch baking dish and transfer to the oven. Remove the dish when the butter has melted.

   In a bowl, stir together the flour and sugar, then pour in the milk, and stir to combine. The batter will have a few lumps, but that's okay. Pour the batter into the dish on top of the melted butter.

   Spoon the fruit on top of the batter and then slowly pour the fruit juice on top of that. Be careful not to mix the fruit into the batter, though. If desired, sprinkle with the cinnamon. Bake until golden brown on top and the fruit is bubbling, 35 to 45 minutes. Serve warm.

serves 12

 BLUE rIBBON TIP Cobblers cook best in light, not dark, baking pans. Glass is my first choice, so you can see the fruit bubbling away, and I am partial to oblong or rectangular dishes as opposed to big round ones, where the centers don't get as much heat.

CATCH-A-HUSBAND BLACKBERRY COBBLER

My soda biscuits and blackberry cobbler got me a husband, and that's the real truth. My first dinner for Mark, I made this and it turned out blackberry cobbler was his absolute favorite dessert in the world. He proposed four weeks later. No matter how many award-winning pies, cookies, bars, or cakes I'd make, he'd go for blackberry cobbler every time—I swear he'd rather eat it than a steak. This recipe serves a big table of people, unless, of course, you're at my house, in which case I got to make one for the husband and one for everybody else!

INGREDIENTS

- 4 tablespoons (½ stick) unsalted butter
- 1½ cups Bisquick baking mix
- ⅔ cup whole milk
- ⅔ cup granulated sugar
- 1 (15-ounce) can blackberry pie filling (see Blue Ribbon Tip, below)
- 1 teaspoon packed light brown sugar

DIRECTIONS

Preheat the oven to 350°F. While the oven is heating, put the butter in an 8-inch square baking dish and transfer to the oven. Remove the dish when the butter has melted.

In a medium bowl, stir together the Bisquick, milk, and granulated sugar until smooth. Pour into the dish on top of the butter. Drop spoonfuls of the pie filling over the batter. Do not stir. Sprinkle the brown sugar over the top of the mixture.

Bake until golden brown on top, 30 to 35 minutes. Serve warm.

SERVES 8 TO 10

 BLUE RIBBON TIP Living down here, we're lucky because we're close to all the orchards and farmer's markets, so we get great fruit. In summer, I simmer 4 cups fresh blackberries with ½ cup sugar until thick and use in place of the pie filling.

HONEY BUN CAKE

Friends are always calling me up, telling me their favorite baked goods, and then wanting me to turn them into a different dessert. A few years back, a girlfriend of mine called me up, talking about how much she just loved Little Debbie Honey Buns and how she wanted to make a cake that tasted like them. It took me fifteen different tries to get this just right—real sweet and sticky. Now, my friend makes this every single Sunday for her family.

INGREDIENTS

cake

- ¾ cup (1½ sticks) unsalted butter, melted, plus more for the pan
- All-purpose flour, for the pan
- 1 (15-ounce) box yellow cake mix
- 4 large eggs
- 1 cup sour cream

filling

- 1 cup firmly packed light brown sugar
- ½ cup chopped pecans (optional)
- 1 tablespoon ground cinnamon

glaze

- 3 cups confectioner's sugar
- ½ cup whole milk
- 2 teaspoons pure vanilla extract

DIRECTIONS

Preheat the oven to 325°F. Grease and flour a 9 × 13-inch baking pan.

Make the cake: Using an electric mixer, combine the cake mix, eggs, sour cream, and butter. Mix on medium speed until thick, about 2 minutes. Pour enough batter into the pan to come one-quarter of the way up the sides.

Prepare the filling: In a small bowl, combine the brown sugar, pecans (if using), and cinnamon and then sprinkle over the cake batter. Cover with the remaining cake batter.

Bake until a cake tester or toothpick inserted in the center of the cake comes out clean, 40 to 45 minutes.

Make the glaze: Whisk together the confectioner's sugar, milk, and vanilla extract. While the cake is still hot, poke holes in it. Pour the glaze over the hot cake. Let the cake cool on a wire rack before serving warm or at room temperature.

MAKES ONE 9 × 13-INCH CAKE

CHOCOLATE COBBLER

The first time I ever had a chocolate cobbler was at a homecoming dinner at church. This little eighty-something-year-old woman had brought a dessert that looked like a fudge cake in a pan. "No, honey," she said to me, "this is a chocolate cobbler." I asked for the recipe, and, of course, she gave me the wrong thing. (Sometimes people are funny about sharing recipes.) So I searched high and low and had to cook more than a dozen different versions until I hit on this one. We eat this plain because it's just so rich. You ain't lived until you tried this.

INGREDIENTS

- 5 tablespoons unsalted butter, melted, plus more for the pan
- 1¼ cups granulated sugar
- 1 cup all-purpose flour
- 7 tablespoons unsweetened cocoa powder
- 2 teaspoons baking powder
- ¼ teaspoon salt
- ½ cup whole milk
- 1½ teaspoons pure vanilla extract
- ½ cup firmly packed light brown sugar
- 1¼ cups very hot water

DIRECTIONS

Preheat the oven to 350°F. Grease an 8-inch square baking dish.

In a large bowl, stir together ¾ cup of the granulated sugar, the flour, 3 tablespoons of the cocoa powder, the baking powder, and salt. Stir in the milk, butter, and the vanilla extract, mixing until smooth. Pour the batter into the baking dish.

In a separate bowl, stir together the remaining ½ cup granulated sugar, the brown sugar, and the remaining 4 tablespoons cocoa powder. Sprinkle evenly over the batter. Pour the hot water over the top. Do not stir.

Bake until the center is almost set, 35 to 40 minutes. Let stand for 15 minutes before serving.

serves 10

apple crisp

This easy apple crisp is like a pie without the crust. I bring this to any sort of fall get-together, from potlucks to dinner with my in-laws. It's real good with a cup of hot coffee and a scoop of vanilla ice cream. Use whatever baking apples are available, such as Granny Smith, Golden Delicious, Cameo, or Fuji. Just do not use McIntosh—it's the worst apple for baking because it just up and disappears when you cook it! You can put some fresh or dried cranberries or raisins in this one if you're feeling like changing things up.

INGREDIENTS

- ½ cup (1 stick) unsalted butter, at room temperature, plus more for the pan
- 6 cups sliced peeled baking apples (about 6 large)
- ½ cup granulated sugar
- 2 teaspoons ground cinnamon
- ¾ cup self-rising flour (I use White Lily)
- ½ cup firmly packed dark brown sugar
- ½ teaspoon pure vanilla extract

DIRECTIONS

Preheat the oven to 350°F. Grease an 8-inch square or 1½-quart baking dish.

Put the apples in the baking dish. In a small bowl, stir together the granulated sugar and the cinnamon. Sprinkle over the apples.

In a large bowl, combine the flour, brown sugar, butter, and vanilla. Mix with a spoon until you get a crumbly mixture and all the ingredients are incorporated. Evenly spoon the mixture over the apples.

Bake until the apples are tender and the topping is golden brown, 35 to 45 minutes. Serve warm.

serves 8 to 10

SOUTHERN RICE PUDDING

Rice pudding is a poor man's dessert—cheap to make, and quick to eat. And everybody I know loves it. In fact, when I first got married, I asked Daddy to make it to have at the wedding, and he did—for 300 people! You can serve this warm or cold, which is how my family likes it, topped with whipped cream and a sprinkle of cinnamon.

INGREDIENTS

½ cup long-grain rice
½ cup raisins
2 large eggs
½ cup sugar

2½ cups whole milk
1¼ teaspoons pure vanilla extract
¼ teaspoon salt

1½ teaspoons ground cinnamon, plus more for serving
Whipped cream, for serving

DIRECTIONS

Preheat the oven to 325°F.

Bring the rice and 1 cup water to a boil in a saucepan, stirring once or twice. Add the raisins, then reduce the heat to low, and simmer, covered, until all the water is absorbed, about 14 minutes. Do not lift the cover to peek during this time.

Using a fork, beat the eggs in a 1½-quart ungreased baking dish. Beat in the sugar, then stir in the milk, vanilla, salt, and hot rice with raisins. Sprinkle the top with the cinnamon and bake, uncovered, stirring every 15 minutes, for 45 minutes. The top will still be wet and not set. Do not overbake, or the mixture will curdle.

Stir the pudding well and allow to stand for 15 minutes. This is when the liquid will be absorbed and the pudding will become creamy. Serve warm or cold, topped with whipped cream and more cinnamon, if you like.

serves 8 to 10

CHOCOLATE CHIP–PEANUT BUTTER PAN CAKE

This is a good, intense chocolate cake. It's a simple thing to make, which is real helpful when you're needing a chocolate fix, but don't want to fuss, and you can put it together in advance, to boot. You can use the frosting on any kind of cake you like—caramel, vanilla, chocolate, or anything that works with peanut butter.

INGREDIENTS

cake

- 4 tablespoons (½ stick) unsalted butter, at room temperature, plus more for the pan
- 1 cup all-purpose flour
- ¼ teaspoon baking powder
- ¼ teaspoon baking soda
- ¼ teaspoon salt
- ½ cup firmly packed light brown sugar
- ⅓ cup creamy peanut butter (I use Jif)
- 1 large egg
- 1 large egg yolk
- ¼ cup sour cream
- ¼ cup hot water
- ½ teaspoon pure vanilla extract
- ½ cup semisweet chocolate chips

frosting

- 5 ounces semisweet chocolate, coarsely chopped
- ½ cup heavy cream
- 1 tablespoon unsalted butter
- 2 tablespoons creamy peanut butter (I use Jif)
- 2 tablespoons granulated sugar

DIRECTIONS

Preheat the oven to 325°F. Grease a 9 × 13-inch baking dish.

Make the cake: In a large bowl, whisk together the flour, baking powder, baking soda, and salt.

Using an electric mixer, on medium speed, blend the brown sugar, peanut butter, and butter until creamy, about 2 minutes. Add the egg and egg yolk and mix for another 2 minutes. Scrape down the sides of the bowl and mix for another minute. Add half of the flour mixture and mix until incorporated, about 20 seconds. Then add the sour cream, mixing again for 20 seconds. Gradually add the remaining flour mixture. Add the hot water in a slow, steady stream and mix on low speed to combine, about 30 seconds. Add the vanilla extract and mix just until incorporated. The batter will be smooth and thick.

Using a rubber spatula, stir in the chocolate chips. Pour the batter into the prepared baking dish, spreading the top evenly.

Bake until a cake tester or toothpick inserted in the center of the cake comes out clean, 22 to 27 minutes. Let cool completely in the dish on a wire rack.

Make the frosting: Put the chocolate in a bowl.

Heat the cream, butter, peanut butter, and granulated sugar in a saucepan over medium heat until the butter and peanut butter are melted. When hot, stir to dissolve the sugar. Bring to a boil, then remove from the heat, and pour over the chocolate. Wait for 5 minutes for the chocolate to melt and then stir the mixture until smooth. Refrigerate until spreadable, 5 to 10 minutes.

Spread the frosting over the top of the cake.

MAKES ONE 9 × 13-INCH CAKE

BLUEBERRY-LEMON STREUSEL BARS

I love anything with lemon in it, and blueberries and lemon go together something perfect, especially in summer. This recipe was sent to me a few years ago by a friend, who clipped it from *Fine Cooking* magazine, and it's a good one to make for a snack or a bake sale or a baby shower.

INGREDIENTS

- 1 cup (2 sticks) unsalted butter, at room temperature, plus more for the pan
- 3 cups all-purpose flour
- 1½ cups old-fashioned rolled oats (not quick oats)
- 1⅓ cups firmly packed light brown sugar
- 1 teaspoon salt
- 1 teaspoon baking powder
- 1 large egg white
- 1 (14-ounce) can sweetened condensed milk
- 2 teaspoons grated lemon zest
- ½ cup fresh lemon juice
- 1 large egg yolk
- 2½ cups (about 13 ounces) blueberries, at room temperature (see Blue Ribbon Tip, page 158)

DIRECTIONS

Preheat the oven to 350°F. Line a 9 × 13-inch baking dish with foil, leaving a 1-inch overhang on the ends. Lightly butter the foil.

In a large bowl, combine the flour, oats, brown sugar, salt, and baking powder. Using your fingers, blend in the butter; the mixture will be crumbly. Transfer half of the crumb mixture to another bowl and reserve for the topping.

Using an electric mixer, blend the egg white into the remaining crumbs and then press the mixture onto the bottom of the pan to form a level crust. Bake until the crust starts to form a dry top, 10 to 12 minutes. Remove the crust, but keep the oven on.

In a medium bowl, whisk the condensed milk, lemon zest, lemon juice, and egg yolk. Let stand for 5 minutes; it will begin to thicken.

recipe continues

Sprinkle the blueberries evenly over the hot crust and then drop spoonfuls of the lemon mixture on top. Spread gently with a spatula, but don't crush the berries; it's fine if the lemon mixture isn't perfectly even. Bake until the lemon mixture just begins to form a shiny skin, 7 to 8 minutes. Remove the baking dish, but keep the oven on.

Press the reserved topping into small lumps and sprinkle them over the blueberry layer. Bake until the filling is bubbling at the edges and the topping is browned, 25 to 30 minutes.

Let cool in the pan on a wire rack until just warm, about 1 hour. Carefully lift out of the pan using the foil overhang and then let cool completely on the rack. Cut into 24 bars. The bars may be stored at room temperature for a few hours, but otherwise should be kept in the refrigerator.

MaKeS 24 BarS

 BLUE rIBBON TIP Be sure to use room-temperature berries. Cold fruit straight from the refrigerator will prevent your dessert from baking evenly.

CHEATER'S CARAMEL APPLE DUMP CAKE

If you think you can't make a cake, this is one you can make, I promise. It's a cheater recipe, done with premade ingredients that you just dump together. This is also one to pull out when you're needing to save; since almost everything is jarred or canned, you might already have what you need in the pantry and won't have to go buying lots of ingredients. The butter will melt into the apples, creating the juices and making a real good cold-weather-time cake.

INGREDIENTS

- ½ cup (1 stick) unsalted butter, sliced and slightly softened, plus more for the pan
- 1 cup thinly sliced peeled Granny Smith apples

- 1 (16-ounce) can apple pie filling
- ½ cup apple juice
- ¼ cup firmly packed light brown sugar
- 2 tablespoons ground cinnamon

- 4 ounces cream cheese, cut into chunks, at room temperature
- ¼ cup chopped pecans
- ½ cup caramel topping
- 1 (15-ounce) box yellow cake mix

DIRECTIONS

Preheat the oven to 350°F. Grease a 9 × 13-inch baking dish.

Put the apple slices into the baking dish. Pour the apple pie filling and apple juice on top and then sprinkle 2 tablespoons of the brown sugar and 1 tablespoon of the cinnamon over the apple mixture. Scatter the cream cheese chunks on top, sprinkle with the pecans, and drizzle with the caramel topping. Pour the dry cake mix over everything and top with the pats of butter. Sprinkle with the remaining 2 tablespoons brown sugar and 1 tablespoon cinnamon.

Bake until golden brown on top, 35 to 40 minutes. Let cool at least slightly on a wire rack. Serve warm or at room temperature.

MAKES ONE 9 × 13-INCH CAKE

German Upside-Down Cake

Regular German chocolate cake's too much cake and not enough frosting for me. So I messed around with it a little bit, like I always do, adding cream cheese, pecans, and more coconut, and came up with this. When you flip the cake over, you get lots of that good tasty topping.

INGREDIENTS

- ½ cup (1 stick) unsalted butter or margarine, at room temperature, plus more for the pan
- All-purpose flour, for the pan
- 1 cup sweetened coconut flakes
- 1 cup chopped pecans
- 1 (18.25-ounce) package German chocolate cake mix
- Eggs, oil, and water as directed on package
- 1 (8-ounce) package cream cheese, at room temperature
- 2 cups confectioner's sugar

DIRECTIONS

Preheat the oven to 350°F. Grease and flour a 9 × 13-inch baking dish and set it on a baking sheet.

Sprinkle the coconut and pecans evenly over the bottom of the prepared baking dish. Prepare the cake mix following the package directions, with the appropriate measurements of eggs, oil, and water. Pour the cake batter into the dish.

Using an electric mixer, beat together the cream cheese, butter, and confectioner's sugar. Drop by spoonfuls over the top of the cake batter.

Bake until a cake tester or toothpick inserted in the center of the cake comes out clean, 45 to 50 minutes. Let the cake cool completely in the baking dish on a wire rack. Flip over and unmold onto a serving plate before slicing.

MAKES ONE 9 × 13-INCH CAKE

GraNNY'S applesauce Cake

This here's a good back-to-school cake. Granny used to make this every fall, with her good homemade applesauce. Sometimes she'd frost it or drizzle it with caramel sauce, but most of the time she'd just sprinkle some powdered sugar on there. This is an old pan measurement; if you didn't inherit one of these pans from your granny, you can use a 9 × 13-inch baking dish, but the cake will bake more quickly and will be thinner.

INGREDIENTS

- ½ cup (1 stick) unsalted butter, plus more for the pan
- 2 cups all-purpose flour
- 1 teaspoon baking soda
- 1 teaspoon ground cinnamon
- ¼ teaspoon ground cloves
- Pinch of salt
- 1 cup sugar
- 1 large egg
- 1 cup applesauce
- 1 cup raisins
- 1 cup chopped walnuts

DIRECTIONS

Preheat the oven to 350°F. Grease a 9 × 11-inch pan.

Sift together the flour, baking soda, cinnamon, cloves, and salt. Using an electric mixer, beat together the butter and sugar until fluffy and pale. Add the egg and beat well, then alternately add the flour mixture and the applesauce, mixing well until the ingredients are combined; the mixture will be smooth and thin. Stir in the raisins and nuts and pour into the pan.

Bake until golden brown, about 1 hour and 15 minutes. Let cool completely in the pan on a wire rack.

MaKeS ONe 9 × 11-INCH CaKe

CROCK-POT MONKEY BREAD

These days, everybody and their mama's out buying a slow cooker. But did you know you can also bake in it? This is a simple and tasty monkey bread recipe, and a Crock-Pot makes it even easier. The icing is good for honey buns, pound cake, apple bread, pumpkin bread—anything you might want to glaze.

INGREDIENTS

- ½ cup (1 stick) unsalted butter or margarine, melted
- 1 (8-ounce) tube jumbo-sized refrigerated biscuits (8 biscuits), cold
- 1 cup firmly packed light brown sugar
- 1 tablespoon ground cinnamon
- 2 cups confectioner's sugar
- 1 to 2½ teaspoons whole milk or heavy cream

DIRECTIONS

Use some of the butter to grease the inside of your slow cooker. Cut each biscuit into quarters. In a small bowl, combine the brown sugar and cinnamon.

Dip each biscuit into the melted butter and then the cinnamon-sugar, before arranging in a single layer on the bottom of the slow cooker. It's okay if the biscuits touch. Cover and cook on high for 2 hours.

Whisk together the confectioner's sugar and 1 teaspoon milk in a bowl. Add additional milk until you have a smooth icing.

Remove the slow cooker lid and let the bread cool for a few minutes. Flip the monkey bread onto a clean plate or tray. The bread will be browned and puffed up. Drizzle with the icing and serve warm.

7UP Cake

7UP cake is a Southern go-to and something almost everybody down here knows how to make. It's a real moist Bundt cake that you make when you want to whip up something comforting and easy, like for a funeral or church gathering. I don't make it too much now, since I ate it so much growing up, but it's a great classic recipe that y'all should know by heart.

INGREDIENTS

cake
- 1½ cups (3 sticks) unsalted butter, at room temperature, plus more for the pan
- 3 cups granulated sugar
- 5 large eggs
- 3 cups all-purpose flour
- 3 teaspoons lemon extract
- 1 teaspoon pure vanilla extract
- ¾ cup 7UP

icing
- 1¼ cups confectioner's sugar
- 2 tablespoons whole milk
- 2 teaspoons lemon extract
- 1 teaspoon pure vanilla extract

DIRECTIONS

Preheat the oven to 325°F. Thoroughly grease a 10-inch Bundt pan.

Make the cake: Using an electric mixer, beat together the butter and granulated sugar on medium-low speed until light and fluffy, about 10 minutes. Add the eggs, one at a time, mixing well after each addition. One ingredient at a time, mix in the flour, lemon extract, and vanilla extract. Using a rubber spatula, fold in the 7UP.

Pour into the pan and bake until a cake tester or toothpick inserted in the center of the cake comes out clean, about 60 minutes. Let cool for 10 minutes on a wire rack.

Make the icing: Whisk together the confectioner's sugar, milk, lemon extract, and vanilla extract until smooth.

Flip the cake over onto a platter and then drizzle with the icing while still warm. Let cool completely before serving.

MAKES ONE 10-INCH BUNDT CAKE

STRAWBERRY-CHOCOLATE TRIFLE

I first made this recipe a few years back for a strawberry festival here in South Carolina. I came up with this because I needed something that could travel (the festival's a three-hour drive) and that if they didn't like, I could still eat. I ended up winning, so you know it's a real good dessert! I like it best with yellow cake because you already have the sweetness of the strawberries and the chocolate pudding, but it's good with chocolate cake, too. It's an amazing summer dessert and looks real dainty and nice piled up in that big bowl.

INGREDIENTS

- ⅓ cup vegetable oil, plus more for the pan
- 1 (18-ounce) box yellow cake mix or chocolate cake mix
- 3 large eggs
- 1 large (8.5-ounce) box chocolate pudding mix (not instant)
- 3 cups whole milk
- 1 cup heavy cream
- 1 teaspoon pure vanilla extract
- ½ cup confectioner's sugar
- 4 cups sliced fresh strawberries

DIRECTIONS

Preheat the oven to 350°F. Grease a 10 × 15-inch jelly roll pan.

Using an electric mixer, beat together the cake mix, 1 cup water, the oil, and eggs on medium speed for 2 minutes. Pour the batter into the pan.

Bake until a cake tester or toothpick inserted in the center of the cake comes out clean and the cake begins to come away from the sides of the pan, 20 to 25 minutes. Let cool completely on a wire rack.

In a heavy saucepan, combine the pudding mix and milk and whisk until combined. Cook over medium heat, whisking constantly, until the mixture thickens and comes to a boil. Remove from the heat and let cool for 30 minutes, stirring occasionally.

Using an electric mixer, whip the cream, vanilla extract, and confectioner's sugar until stiff peaks form.

Cut the cooled cake into 1-inch pieces and put half of them on the bottom of a large glass bowl. Pour half of the cooled pudding over the cake pieces and top with half of the strawberries. Repeat the layers and then top with the whipped cream. Cover and refrigerate for at least 2 hours or overnight before serving. Store any leftovers, covered, in the refrigerator.

serves 12

chapter

6

BAKED GOODS TO SHOW OFF

CHOCOLATE WHOOPIE CAKE

UPSIDE-DOWN APPLE-PECAN PIE

WORLD-FAMOUS CHOCOLATE BACON PEANUT BUTTER PIE

LEMON TIRAMISÙ

DEATH BY CHOCOLATE CAKE

BOURBON-PECAN PIE

UPSIDE-DOWN PEAR CAKE

PRALINE CHEESECAKE

CREAM PUFFS

TURTLE CAKE ROLL

CLASSIC CARAMEL CAKE

Chocolate Whoopie Cake

My daughter, Sarablake, loves chocolate, and when I finished making this for her tenth birthday, she said, "Mama, that's just one big ol' whoopie pie." We are whoopie pie fans, me and the family, so the name stuck and now I end up making this chocolate cake with whipped cream frosting and chocolate icing a whole lot.

INGREDIENTS

cake

- ⅔ cup vegetable oil, plus more for the pans
- 1 cup well-shaken buttermilk (see Blue Ribbon Tip, page 22)
- 2 cups granulated sugar
- 3 large eggs
- 2 cups all-purpose flour
- ¾ cup unsweetened cocoa powder
- 1 teaspoon baking soda
- ½ teaspoon salt
- ½ teaspoon espresso powder

filling

- 2 cups heavy cream
- 6 ounces cream cheese
- 1 cup confectioner's sugar

icing

- 1 cup heavy cream
- 8 ounces semisweet chocolate, chopped (or chocolate chips)

DIRECTIONS

Preheat the oven to 350°F. Grease two 9-inch round cake pans, line the bottoms with parchment paper, and grease the paper.

Make the cake: In a medium bowl, whisk together the buttermilk, 1 cup water, the oil, granulated sugar, and eggs until well blended. Sift together the flour, cocoa powder, baking soda, salt, and espresso powder. Add the egg mixture and whisk to combine, making sure there are no lumps. Do not overbeat. Divide the batter evenly between the pans.

Bake until a cake tester or toothpick inserted in the center of the cake comes out clean, 30 to 35 minutes. Let cool in the pans for 10 minutes and then unmold the cakes onto wire racks to cool completely. Peel off the parchment paper.

Prepare the filling: Using an electric mixer, whip the cream until soft peaks form. You'll need the mixer to beat the cream cheese and confectioner's sugar, so transfer the cream to a new bowl if you're using a stand mixer; there's no need to clean the bowl or beater(s), though. Beat together the cream cheese and confectioner's sugar until creamy and smooth. Using a rubber spatula, gently fold in the whipped cream.

Put one of the cakes on a cake platter domed side down. Spoon all of the whipped cream mixture onto the cake (it will be a thick layer). Put the other cake on top domed side up. Your cake should resemble a giant whoopie pie.

Make the icing: Heat the cream and chocolate in a microwave or double boiler, stirring until the chocolate has melted and the mixture is smooth. Let cool slightly, so that the mixture is not too warm, but still pourable.

Pour the icing over the cake and smooth the top using the back of a large spoon. The icing should drip over the sides of the cake.

MAKES ONE 9-INCH LAYER CAKE

UPSIDE-DOWN APPLE-PECAN PIE

This is the pie that made me famous in the pie world, my first North Carolina Grand Champion–winning recipe, which has since been featured in magazines and made by probably hundreds of people. Here's the story: I was getting ready for a competition just a week before my wedding. I had been fixing to make something else, but Mark tried this pie and said it was the one I should enter. And would you believe it? I ended up with that big ol' blue ribbon. It was a good luck charm for my wedding, too, I think. People sometimes think this pie is fake because the nuts on top are just so shiny and gorgeous. It's a showstopper.

INGREDIENTS

- ½ cup (1 stick) unsalted butter, at room temperature
- 3 tablespoons all-purpose flour, plus more for rolling
- 2 (9-inch) store-bought refrigerated pie crusts (see Blue Ribbon Tip, page 172)
- About 1½ cups pecan halves
- 1½ cups firmly packed light brown sugar
- ½ cup granulated sugar
- 1 tablespoon apple pie spice
- 1⅛ teaspoons ground cinnamon
- ½ teaspoon ground nutmeg
- 2 tablespoons fresh lemon juice
- 1 teaspoon pure vanilla extract
- 6 cups sliced peeled baking apples

DIRECTIONS

Preheat the oven to 450°F. Thoroughly grease a 10-inch deep-dish ceramic pie pan (you must use a deep-dish pan) with all of the butter.

On a lightly floured surface, roll each of the pie crusts until about 11 inches in diameter. Transfer to baking sheets and refrigerate until needed.

Starting on the bottom and working your way outside in, arrange the pecans, round side down, in the pan, covering it entirely and making sure there are very few gaps in between the nuts. Do the same up the sides, too. Spread the brown sugar over the nuts until they are entirely covered and then press one of the pie crusts down

recipe continues

firmly on top of the nuts, making sure that the nuts do not poke through.

In a bowl, stir together the flour, granulated sugar, apple pie spice, cinnamon, nutmeg, lemon juice, and vanilla extract. Add the apples and toss to coat. Pour the apples into the pie crust as evenly as possible. Cover with the second pie crust. Fold the crust sides over each other and crimp together firmly. Don't worry too much about appearances, as this will be the bottom of your pie. Using a fork, poke a few holes in the crust.

Bake for 10 minutes, then reduce the oven temperature to 350°F, and continue to bake until browned, about 45 minutes. Remove from the oven and let the pie sit just until the bubbling stops, 3 to 4 minutes. Flip the pie out onto a serving dish while still hot—the pecans on top of the pie should be very shiny, and all the pastry should be covered. Serve warm.

MAKES ONE 10-INCH DEEP-DISH PIE

 BLUE RIBBON TIP Store-bought pie crusts (I like Pillsbury) work best here because they're sturdier than homemade and can hold up to all the heaviness from the apples and nuts.

WORLD-FAMOUS CHOCOLATE BACON PEANUT BUTTER PIE

This pie's been all over the world, shared and linked to and whatnot eight million times. One of my fans found the recipe on my Facebook page and brought it to a hotel where she was vacationing in Belize. The chef there liked it so much, she put it on the menu, and now they're serving *my* pie at a fancy resort in Belize! I made this on national television and me and my crazy redneck ideas changed a British master baker's mind about American flavors. Rich chocolate, crunchy cookies, that smoky bacon flavor, smooth cream cheese, and, of course, nutty peanut butter all taste amazing together.

INGREDIENTS

- 5 tablespoons unsalted butter, plus more for the pan
- 1 (16-ounce) package of bacon
- 25 Chips Ahoy! cookies, finely crushed
- ½ cup evaporated milk
- ¾ cup granulated sugar
- 1 (12-ounce) bag semisweet chocolate chips
- 1½ tablespoons vanilla butter and nut flavoring (see Blue Ribbon Tip, page 23)
- 1 (8-ounce) package cream cheese, at room temperature
- 1 cup confectioner's sugar
- 2½ cups heavy cream
- 1 cup extra-crunchy peanut butter (I use Jif)
- Pinch of cream of tartar

DIRECTIONS

Preheat the oven to 350°F. Grease a 10-inch deep-dish pie pan.

Cook the bacon until crisp, either in the microwave for 3½ minutes or on the stovetop. Drain on paper towels before cutting into small pieces.

Melt 3 tablespoons of the butter and mix with the cookie crumbs. Press into the bottom and all the way up the sides of the pie pan. Bake until set, 8 to 11 minutes. Let cool completely on a wire rack.

In a saucepan, heat the evaporated milk and granulated sugar over

recipe continues

medium heat. Add the chocolate chips and stir over medium heat until the mixture is thick, the sugar has dissolved, and the chocolate is completely melted. Remove from the heat and add the remaining 2 tablespoons butter and the vanilla butter and nut flavoring. Set aside to cool, about 15 minutes.

Spread 1½ cups of the chocolate sauce over the crust and let set.

Using an electric mixer, beat together the cream cheese and ½ cup of the confectioner's sugar until smooth. Add 1 cup of the cream and whip until the mixture is fluffy. Add the peanut butter and whip until combined.

Sprinkle half of the bacon over the chocolate-covered crust and then pour in the peanut butter mixture. Sprinkle half of the remaining bacon bits over the peanut butter mixture, then top with half of the remaining chocolate sauce. Whip the remaining 1½ cups heavy cream, the remaining ½ cup confectioner's sugar, and the cream of tartar until stiff, but still smooth. Do not overwhip, or the cream will become grainy. Spread the cream over the pie and pipe on the edges, if desired. Sprinkle with the remaining bacon and drizzle the rest of the chocolate sauce on top. Refrigerate for at least 1 hour or overnight before serving.

MAKES ONE 10-INCH DEEP-DISH PIE

LEMON TIRAMISÙ

I learned how to make this lemon tiramisù in high school home economics class. We were trying to come up with "desserts that impressed people" and this one's real impressive. I love tiramisù and I love lemon, so I figured why the heck not? This is real creamy, but also refreshing when you use lemon in place of the usual coffee. And it won't keep you up all night! There's a bunch of egg yolks in this, since you're making a lemon curd, so save the leftover egg whites and use them for meringues.

INGREDIENTS

- 1¼ cups sugar
- 1 tablespoon grated lemon zest
- ¾ cup fresh lemon juice
- 6 large egg yolks
- ¼ cup all-purpose flour

- 2 cups whole milk
- 4 tablespoons (½ stick) unsalted butter, cubed
- 2 ounces white chocolate, finely chopped

- 1½ cups heavy cream
- 1 cup mascarpone cheese, at room temperature
- 24 to 26 ladyfinger cookies, as needed

DIRECTIONS

In a small saucepan, stir together ½ cup of the sugar, ½ cup of the lemon juice, and ½ cup water over medium heat until dissolved, about 5 minutes. Set the lemon syrup aside to cool.

In a large heatproof bowl, whisk together the egg yolks, flour, and the remaining ¾ cup sugar until smooth and pale.

In a heavy-bottomed saucepan, heat the milk over medium heat just until bubbles appear around the edges. Whisking vigorously, add half of the hot milk to the egg yolk mixture,

making sure not to scramble the yolks. Whisk everything back into the milk in the pan. Cook, whisking the whole time, until boiling and thickened, about 10 minutes. Remove from the heat and mix in the butter and white chocolate. Strain through a fine-mesh sieve into a bowl. Stir in the lemon zest and the remaining ¼ cup lemon juice. Press plastic wrap directly onto the surface of the custard mixture and refrigerate until cold, about 2 hours.

Using an electric mixer, whip the cream until it holds stiff peaks.

Whisk the mascarpone into the chilled custard and then use a rubber spatula to fold in the whipped cream.

Arrange half of the ladyfinger cookies in a 9 × 13-inch glass baking dish. Generously brush the cookies with half of the lemon syrup. Spread with half of the cream mixture. Repeat with the remaining ladyfingers, syrup, and cream. Cover and refrigerate for at least 4 hours and up to 6 before serving.

SERVES 10 TO 12

 COFFEE TIRAMISÙ You can change this from lemon to regular (but still alcohol-free) by omitting the lemon zest and juice and replacing it with 2 teaspoons dark espresso powder to make the syrup for brushing the cookies. Top with a simple chocolate ganache (see page 97) and you'll have all the flavors of a more traditional tiramisù.

Death by Chocolate Cake

This is just an amazing cake—buttermilk makes it real moist and the coffee brings out all the chocolate flavors. This cake's good for a celebration or any time you really got a hankering for chocolate. A girlfriend of mine asked me to make this when she got divorced, and we put a little bride and groom on top and just cut that groom's head right off! It doesn't make everything better, but it sure tastes good. If you can, use high-quality chocolate—it really makes this cake.

INGREDIENTS

cake
- ¾ cup vegetable oil, plus more for the pans
- 3 ounces semisweet chocolate, chopped
- 1½ cups coffee, hot
- 3 cups granulated sugar
- 2½ cups all-purpose flour
- 1½ cups unsweetened cocoa powder
- 2 teaspoons baking soda
- ¾ teaspoon baking powder
- 1¼ teaspoons salt
- 3 large eggs
- 1½ cups well-shaken buttermilk (see Blue Ribbon Tip, page 22)
- ¾ teaspoon pure vanilla extract

frosting
- 1½ cups (3 sticks) unsalted butter, at room temperature
- 1 cup unsweetened cocoa powder
- 4½ cups confectioner's sugar
- ½ to ¾ cup heavy cream, as needed
- 1½ teaspoons pure vanilla extract

DIRECTIONS

Preheat the oven to 300°F. Grease three 9-inch square or round cake pans, line with parchment paper, and then grease the paper.

Make the cake: Put the chocolate in a heat-resistant bowl. Pour the hot coffee over the chocolate and let sit, stirring occasionally, until the chocolate is melted and the mixture is smooth.

In a large bowl, sift together the granulated sugar, flour, cocoa powder, baking soda, baking powder, and salt. Using an electric mixer, beat the eggs until slightly thickened and lemon colored, 3 to 5 minutes. Slowly add the oil, buttermilk, vanilla extract, and melted chocolate mixture and mix until combined. Add the flour mixture and beat on medium speed until just combined.

Divide the batter among the pans and bake until a cake tester or toothpick inserted in the center of the cake comes out clean, 35 to 45 minutes. Let cool completely in the pans on wire racks. Run a thin knife around the edges of the pans and invert the layers onto the racks. Peel off the parchment paper.

Prepare the frosting: Using an electric mixer, beat the butter on medium-high speed until smooth and fluffy, 2 to 3 minutes. Mix in the cocoa powder. Add ½ cup of the confectioner's sugar and mix well. Continue adding confectioner's sugar, ½ cup at a time, mixing well after each addition. As the frosting thickens, start adding the cream a few tablespoons at a time, alternating with the sugar. Once all of the sugar has been added, whip until the frosting is light and fluffy. Mix in the vanilla.

Before frosting the cake, use a large serrated knife to carefully level off the top of each cake layer so it is completely flat. Put one layer on a cake plate and spread ½ cup of the frosting on top. Put the second layer on top and spread with ½ cup of the frosting. Add the final cake layer and then cover the entire cake with a thin layer of frosting. Refrigerate the cake to set the thin layer of frosting, about 15 minutes. Remove the cake from the refrigerator and cover with the remaining frosting, piping some of it on decoratively, if you like.

MAKES ONE 9-INCH LAYER CAKE

 BLUE RIBBON TIP When frosting a cake, I like to do a crumb coat: Spread a very thin layer of frosting over all of it and then refrigerate to set. This will make the frosting easier to spread on the cake and will keep pesky crumbs from mixing into your pretty frosting.

Bourbon-Pecan Pie

This one started out as a screw-up and ended up as one of my most impressive pies. I even won my local summertime pie bake-off with this recipe—even though the edges were burnt! The pie ends up looking real cool: the pecan filling floats to the top while the cheesecake stays at the bottom. Now, I'm no bourbon drinker, but I just love the way it tastes with nuts when you cook them together.

INGREDIENTS

1¾ cups sugar

1 (8-ounce) package cream cheese, at room temperature

3 large eggs

1 tablespoon pure vanilla extract

1 unbaked 10-inch deep-dish pie crust

1½ cups chopped pecans

4 tablespoons (½ stick) unsalted butter, melted

¾ cup light corn syrup

1 tablespoon bourbon

DIRECTIONS

Preheat the oven to 375°F.

Using an electric mixer, beat together ¾ cup of the sugar and the cream cheese until smooth. Beat in 1 of the eggs and the vanilla extract. Spread in the pie crust. Scatter the pecans on top.

In a medium bowl, whisk the remaining 1 cup sugar, remaining 2 eggs, butter, corn syrup, and bourbon. Pour over the nuts in the pie crust.

Bake until firm in the middle and dark brown on top, 45 to 55 minutes. Let cool completely before serving.

Makes one 10-inch deep-dish pie

UPSIDE-DOWN PEAR CAKE

A friend of mine who loves upside-down cakes sent me this recipe around fifteen years ago. I've experimented with it and tried every kind of pear; Bartletts are the best, I think—juicy and flavorful. This is a rich cake, perfect in fall or winter when sweet pears come out.

INGREDIENTS

- 10 tablespoons (1¼ sticks) unsalted butter, at room temperature, plus more for the pan
- 5 large ripe Bartlett pears, peeled and quartered
- 2 tablespoons fresh lemon juice
- 4 tablespoons granulated sugar
- ¼ cup plus 2 tablespoons bourbon
- 1 cup all-purpose flour
- 1 tablespoon ground ginger
- 1 teaspoon ground cinnamon
- ¼ teaspoon ground cloves
- ¼ teaspoon ground nutmeg
- ¼ teaspoon salt
- ¼ cup firmly packed dark brown sugar
- 3 large eggs
- ½ cup unsulfured molasses
- 1½ tablespoons finely chopped candied ginger
- 1 teaspoon baking soda
- 2 tablespoons boiling water

DIRECTIONS

Preheat the oven to 350°F. Grease a 9-inch round cake pan.

In a large bowl, toss the pears with the lemon juice.

In a large skillet over medium-high heat, melt 2 tablespoons of the butter and then sprinkle 2 tablespoons of the granulated sugar on top. Add half of the pears, cut side down, in a single layer, and cook until browned, 2 to 3 minutes on each side. Remove from the pan with a slotted spoon and transfer to a plate. Add the remaining pears and brown for 2 to 3 minutes per side before transferring to the plate.

Add the bourbon to the pear juices in the skillet and sprinkle in the remaining 2 tablespoons granulated sugar. Cook over medium-high heat, stirring, until reduced to a syrup, about 1 minute. Pour the syrup into the prepared cake pan and swirl to spread. Starting at the edges of the pan, fan out the pears in a single layer.

In a medium bowl, whisk together the flour, ground ginger, cinnamon, cloves, nutmeg, and salt.

Using an electric mixer, beat the remaining 8 tablespoons butter until fluffy. Add the brown sugar and beat on medium-high speed until smooth, about 3 minutes. Add the eggs, one at a time, and beat to combine. Mix in the molasses and candied ginger. Add half of the flour mixture and mix on low speed to combine.

In a small bowl, combine the baking soda and the boiling water. Mix into the batter. Beat in the remaining flour mixture until combined. Pour into the pan over the pears.

Bake for 25 minutes, then reduce the oven temperature to 325°F, and bake until springy to the touch, 15 to 20 minutes. Let cool on a wire rack for 30 minutes. Run a knife around the edges of the pan and then flip the cake onto a serving plate. Serve warm or at room temperature.

MaKes One 9-Inch Cake

praline cheesecake

If you like pralines, try this recipe—they're everywhere! There's praline in the crust and in the filling, and the chocolate sauce brings everything together. Show off this dessert at a party or celebration of some kind.

INGREDIENTS

crust

- 4 tablespoons (½ stick) unsalted butter, melted, plus more for the pan
- 1 cup graham cracker crumbs (about 14 crackers)
- ½ cup finely chopped pecans
- ½ cup firmly packed light brown sugar
- ½ cup chopped English toffee, store-bought or homemade (page 231)

filling

- 4 (8-ounce) packages cream cheese, at room temperature
- 1 cup granulated sugar
- 4 large eggs
- ¼ cup chopped English toffee, store-bought or homemade (page 231)
- ¼ cup finely chopped pecans

sauce

- 4 tablespoons (½ stick) unsalted butter
- ⅔ cup firmly packed light brown sugar
- ⅓ cup heavy cream
- ¼ cup light corn syrup
- 2 ounces bittersweet or semisweet baking chocolate, coarsely chopped
- 1 teaspoon pure vanilla extract

DIRECTIONS

Preheat the oven to 300°F. Grease the bottom and sides of a 9-inch springform pan.

Make the crust: Stir together the graham cracker crumbs, pecans, brown sugar, and butter. Press the mixture evenly into the bottom and 1 inch up the sides of the prepared pan. Bake until set and the edges are lightly browned, 10 to 12 minutes. Remove from the oven and quickly sprinkle with the toffee bits. Set aside to cool.

Prepare the filling: Using an electric mixer, beat the cream cheese and granulated sugar on medium speed until creamy, scraping the sides of the bowl occasionally. Add the eggs, one at a time, and continue beating until combined. Let the filling rest for about 5 minutes to allow air bubbles to rise to the surface.

Pour the filling into the crust and bake until the edges are set and lightly browned and the center wiggles slightly, 65 to 70 minutes.

Immediately sprinkle the toffee and pecans on top of the cheesecake filling and then let cool on a wire rack for 1 hour. Refrigerate, uncovered, until thoroughly chilled, 3 to 4 hours. Cover and return to the refrigerator overnight.

Make the sauce: Melt the butter in a saucepan over medium heat. Stir in the brown sugar, cream, corn syrup, chocolate, and vanilla extract. Cook, stirring occasionally, until the mixture just comes to a boil and the chocolate is melted. Boil and stir for 3 minutes and then remove from the heat. The sauce will be shiny and dark. Set aside to cool.

Loosen the sides of the cheesecake by running a knife around the inside of the pan and then remove the sides. Pour the chocolate sauce over the cheesecake and let set before serving.

MAKES ONE 9-INCH CHEESECAKE

 BLUE RIBBON TIP I'll let y'all in on a little secret of mine: I have this chocolate sauce on hand at all times. I make a double batch, one for the cheesecake and one for pouring over toast slathered in peanut butter. You know those mason jars you use to keep jelly in? They're not just for canning; they're for storage (and iced tea), too. Pour this sauce in a jar and keep it in the back of the fridge for snack time.

CREAM PUFFS

I put this recipe in here for all y'all who are scared of cream puffs. People think making them is this big huge drawn-out process, but I got this recipe simplified to where anybody can make it. If I can make 171 of these little things in an hour, y'all can do at least 22! Cream puffs are nice to bring somewhere as a hostess gift because they look real fancy. If you feel like whipping up some chocolate sauce (see page 185), it makes a nice pairing.

INGREDIENTS

puffs
- ½ cup (1 stick) unsalted butter
- 1¼ cups all-purpose flour

- ⅜ teaspoon salt
- 4 large eggs

filling
- 2 cups heavy cream
- ¼ cup sugar
- 1 teaspoon pure vanilla extract

DIRECTIONS

Preheat the oven to 425°F. Line 2 baking sheets with parchment paper.

Make the puffs: In a medium saucepan, bring 1 cup water and the butter to a rolling boil. Remove the pan from the heat, and add the flour and salt all at once, mixing energetically with a wooden spoon. Return the pan to medium heat and cook, stirring constantly, until the flour is completely mixed in, about 1 minute. Remove from the heat and let cool for 10 minutes.

Transfer the mixture to a large mixing bowl, and using an electric mixer, beat in the eggs, one at a time. Once the last egg has been added, beat for 2 minutes.

Using a ¼ cup measuring cup (or with a piping bag, or a plastic bag with a corner cut off, if you prefer), spoon (or pipe) equal amounts of batter about 2 inches apart on the baking sheets. Bake for 15 minutes, then decrease the oven temperature to 350°F, and bake until golden brown, an additional 12 to 15 minutes. Do not open the oven during this time.

Remove from the oven and cut a small slit in the side of each pastry. Remove from the pans and let cool on wire racks. Once cool, split each puff through the middle so there is a top and bottom section.

Make the filling: Using an electric mixer, whip the cream on high speed and sprinkle in the sugar and vanilla extract gradually. Whip until the cream begins to stiffen and soft peaks form, about 10 minutes.

Fill the bottom halves of the puffs with the whipped cream and then lightly top with the top halves.

MAKES ABOUT 22 CREAM PUFFS

 BLUE RIBBON TIP When making these, you have to use a wooden spoon and you have to just beat the crap out of that batter. And when the puffs are cooking, do not peek, or they will not bake right. Like I always say, "If you looking, you ain't cooking."

TURTLE CAKE ROLL

My Nana always said I had to learn to make a roll cake to impress people. I do think a roll cake is festive, especially when you call it a "roulade," but it takes a lot less time to make than, say, a layer cake. I like messing around with all the possible flavors and combinations, whether it's red velvet or pumpkin with candied ginger or this here turtle roll. If you bake this for Christmas, you can make it look like a fireplace log and cover it with chocolate shavings and those meringue mushrooms.

INGREDIENTS

caramel
- 30 store-bought caramels
- ½ cup heavy cream

cake
- 2 tablespoons vegetable oil, plus more for the pan
- 3 large eggs
- 1¾ cups devil's food cake mix
- 1 tablespoon confectioner's sugar

frosting
- ½ cup heavy cream
- 1 cup milk chocolate chips
- 1¼ tablespoons light corn syrup
- ¼ teaspoon pure vanilla extract
- 1½ cups chopped pecans, toasted

DIRECTIONS

Prepare the caramel: Melt the caramels with the heavy cream in a microwave or double boiler, stirring until smooth. Refrigerate until completely cooled, 2 to 3 hours.

Preheat the oven to 350°F. Line a 10 × 15-inch jelly-roll pan with parchment paper and grease the paper.

Make the cake: Using an electric mixer, beat the eggs on high speed until thick and pale, about 5 minutes. Add the cake mix, oil, and ⅓ cup water, and beat on low speed for 30 seconds and then medium speed for 1 minute, scraping the sides of the bowl occasionally.

Pour into the prepared pan and bake until the cake springs back when lightly touched, but still looks moist, 11 to 14 minutes. Do not overbake, or the cake will be dry and crack when

recipe continues

rolled. Remove from the oven and run a knife around the edges of the pan to make sure the cake does not stick. Lay a clean tea towel on a flat surface and sprinkle with the confectioner's sugar. Turn the cake upside down on the towel and peel off the parchment paper. While hot, carefully roll up the cake in the towel, starting at the short end. Let cool completely on a wire rack, about 1 hour.

Meanwhile, make the frosting: Heat the heavy cream in the microwave or on the stovetop, until it just starts to boil. Stir in the chocolate chips and corn syrup. Let stand for 3 minutes and then whisk until smooth. Mix in the vanilla. Refrigerate, stirring every 15 minutes, until it has a spreadable consistency, about 1 hour.

Once the cake has cooled, remove the caramel from the refrigerator. Using an electric mixer, whip the caramel until it is spreadable and has a frosting-like consistency, about 3 minutes.

Unroll the cake carefully. Spread the caramel evenly over the cake. Reroll the cake, this time without the towel. It should roll easily. Put the cake on a wire rack with a baking sheet underneath to catch any drips. Frost with the chocolate frosting and top with the pecans.

MAKES ONE 10-INCH ROLL

 BLUE RIBBON TIPS Rolling the cake when it's warm makes it easier to roll the second time; it'll mold to the shape you want and won't crack when you roll it again.

Garnish this with a drizzle of salted caramel sauce (see page 125) if you like.

classic caramel cake

Down here, caramel cake's a standard, almost as popular as pound cake. This here's a classic Southern caramel cake, one that has been passed down generation after generation—I know it's been around for at least a hundred years. This one, I just wouldn't screw around with, and I usually screw around with most cakes. It has a lot of steps, I know, and some you just can't avoid—like beating that frosting for a full fifteen minutes. But it's worth it—rich, creamy, and flavored like caramel candy with a dash of vanilla. A candy thermometer is helpful for making the frosting.

INGREDIENTS ....

cake

¾ cup (1½ sticks) unsalted butter, at room temperature, plus more for the pans

3 cups sifted cake flour, plus more for the pans

1 cup whole milk

4 large egg whites, at room temperature

2¼ teaspoons pure vanilla extract

1½ cups sugar

4 teaspoons baking powder

¾ teaspoon salt

¾ cup heavy cream

frosting

3 cups sugar

3 tablespoons light corn syrup

1½ cups whole milk

½ cup (1 stick) unsalted butter, at room temperature

1 teaspoon pure vanilla extract

½ cup heavy cream

DIRECTIONS ....

Preheat the oven to 350°F. Grease and flour three 8-inch round cake pans.

Make the cake: Using an electric mixer, blend ¼ cup of the milk with the egg whites and vanilla extract. In a separate bowl, using an electric mixer, mix the flour, sugar, baking powder, and salt. Add the butter and the remaining ¾ cup milk. Beat at low speed until blended, then beat at

medium speed until smooth, about 1 minute. Beat in the egg white mixture in 3 separate batches.

In another bowl, using an electric mixer with clean beaters, beat the cream until soft peaks form. Stir one-third of the whipped cream into the batter and then use a rubber spatula to fold in the rest. Divide the batter among the pans and smooth the tops.

recipe continues

Bake until a cake tester or toothpick inserted in the center of each cake comes out clean, about 25 minutes. Let the cakes cool in the pans on wire racks for 10 minutes. Unmold the cakes, invert, and let cool completely.

Prepare the frosting: In a saucepan, stir 2½ cups of the sugar with the corn syrup and milk. Cook over medium heat, stirring, until the sugar dissolves. Remove from the heat and keep warm.

Sprinkle the remaining ½ cup sugar into a deep, heavy saucepan. Cook the sugar over medium heat, swirling once it melts, until an amber caramel forms. Carefully pour the warm milk mixture over the caramel. Cook over medium-high heat, stirring, until the caramel dissolves. Stop stirring and cook until the caramel reaches 235°F on a candy thermometer or the soft-ball stage (see Blue Ribbon Tip, below). Remove from the heat. Stir in the butter, vanilla extract, and ¼ cup of the heavy cream. Strain the caramel into a large bowl and let cool for 15 minutes.

Using an electric mixer, beat the caramel on medium speed, gradually adding the remaining ¼ cup cream, until smooth, about 15 minutes.

Set one cake layer on a plate. Pour enough icing over it to cover the top. Top with a second cake layer and cover it with icing. Add the final cake layer and pour the rest of the icing over the top of the cake, letting it run down the sides. Working quickly, use an offset spatula to spread the icing gently around the cake. Let the cake stand at room temperature for 2 hours to set the icing before serving.

MakeS ONe 8-INCH LaYeR CaKe

 BLUe rIBBON TIP If you don't have a candy thermometer, you can test the sugar by dipping a spoon into the hot mixture and dropping a little bit into a cup of cold water. Feel the ball with your fingers to make sure it is the right consistency. For the soft-ball stage, it should form a squishy ball that flattens when you press it between your fingers. For the hard-ball stage, it should form a ball that keeps its shape and won't flatten when you smush it or take it out of the water.

BISCUITS
& BREADS

APPLE PIE BREAD

REDNECK CRACKLIN' CORN
BREAD

PUMPKIN PIE BREAD

EASY-PEASY YEAST BREAD

MAMA'S CORN BREAD

SODA BISCUITS (FOR Y'ALL
WHO THINK YOU CAN'T MAKE
BISCUITS)

BISCUITS LIKE NANA MADE

HOECAKES

JONNYCAKES

CHOCOLATE GRAVY

BLUEBERRY MUFFINS AND A
WAY OF LIFE

CHEESE MUFFINS

CHOCOLATE CHIP CRUMBLE
MUFFINS

DONUT MUFFINS

LEMON STREUSEL MUFFINS

apple pie bread

I came up with this bread for the North Carolina State Apple Festival. Down here in the Carolinas—and we're serious about our apples down here—this was a real big ol' deal. This recipe, which won for the bread division, is one of my all-time favorites. On cold fall days, I get up early, before anyone else, and bake this up for breakfast. That streusel topping is just made to have with coffee.

INGREDIENTS

bread
- ½ cup (1 stick) unsalted butter, at room temperature, plus more for the pan
- 1 cup granulated sugar
- ¼ cup well-shaken buttermilk (see Blue Ribbon Tip, page 22)
- 2 large eggs
- 1 teaspoon pure vanilla extract
- 2 cups self-rising flour (I use White Lily)
- 1 teaspoon apple pie spice
- ½ teaspoon salt
- 2 cups shredded peeled baking apples, preferably a mixture

topping
- ¼ cup firmly packed light brown sugar
- 3 tablespoons all-purpose flour
- 3 tablespoons unsalted butter
- ⅓ cup chopped pecans or walnuts (optional)

DIRECTIONS

Preheat the oven to 350°F. Grease a 9 × 5-inch loaf pan.

Make the bread: Using an electric mixer, beat the butter until smooth. Add the granulated sugar and beat on medium to high speed until light and fluffy. Beat in the buttermilk and then add the eggs, one at a time, and the vanilla extract. Beat until incorporated. Mix in the self-rising flour, apple pie spice, and salt. Stir in the apples. Spoon into the prepared pan.

Prepare the topping: Stir together the brown sugar and all-purpose flour in a small bowl. Using two forks or a pastry cutter, cut in the butter until the mixture resembles coarse crumbs. Stir in the nuts, if using. Sprinkle the streusel topping over the batter.

Bake until light brown on top and a cake tester or toothpick inserted in the center of the bread comes out clean, 60 to 65 minutes. Let cool for 5 minutes in the pan before unmolding onto a wire rack to cool at least slightly. Serve warm or at room temperature.

MAKES ONE 9 × 5-INCH LOAF

redneck cracklin' corn bread

Down here, we like pigs and we like eating pigs. This was Daddy's favorite kind of corn bread, and I just love it, too. This is Mama's recipe, and I recommend you stick to it if you're going to use cracklin's—some corn breads will get real greasy with cracklin's.

INGREDIENTS

- 2 tablespoons shortening (I use Crisco)
- 1½ cups white or yellow cornmeal
- 1 cup all-purpose flour
- 2 teaspoons baking powder
- ½ teaspoon baking soda
- 1 tablespoon sugar
- 1 teaspoon salt
- 1¼ cups well-shaken buttermilk (see Blue Ribbon Tip, page 22)
- 6 tablespoons (¾ stick) unsalted butter, melted
- 1 large egg, lightly beaten
- 1 cup pork cracklin's, larger pieces broken up slightly

DIRECTIONS

Preheat the oven to 400°F. Put the shortening in a 10-inch cast-iron skillet and put it in the oven as it heats.

In a medium bowl, mix together the cornmeal, flour, baking powder, baking soda, sugar, and salt. In a separate bowl, whisk together the buttermilk, butter, and egg. Stir the buttermilk mixture into the flour mixture until just combined. Gently fold in the cracklin's.

Carefully remove the skillet from the oven and pour in the batter. Bake until golden brown on top and a cake tester or toothpick inserted in the center of the bread comes out clean, about 30 minutes. Serve warm.

MAKES ONE 10-INCH CORN BREAD

PUMPKIN PIE BREAD

If you're looking for the perfect basic pumpkin bread recipe, this here's it. Me and Mama came up with this recipe years ago and I have won a lot of contests with it since. You can do almost anything with this bread—cake layers, muffins, coffee cake, even a big fancy roulade. Add nuts, raisins, or mini chocolate chips to it, and it'll hold up just fine. This makes two loaves, one to keep and one to give (or freeze for later).

INGREDIENTS

- 1 cup vegetable oil, plus more for the pans
- 2 cups pure pumpkin puree (from 2 12-ounce cans)
- 2⅔ cups sugar
- 4 large eggs
- 3 cups plus 3 tablespoons all-purpose flour
- 1 teaspoon baking powder
- 1 teaspoon baking soda
- 1 teaspoon salt
- 1½ teaspoons pumpkin pie spice
- ½ teaspoon ground cinnamon

DIRECTIONS

Preheat the oven to 350°F. Grease two 9 × 5-inch loaf pans.

Whisk together the pumpkin, oil, sugar, and eggs. Stir in the flour, baking powder, baking soda, salt, pumpkin pie spice, and cinnamon until well blended. Divide the batter evenly between the prepared pans.

Bake until the top of each loaf is a deep reddish-orange color and springs back when pressed and a cake tester or toothpick inserted in the center of the bread comes out clean, 45 to 50 minutes. Let the loaves cool in the pans on wire racks.

MAKES TWO 9 × 5-INCH LOAVES

easy-peasy yeast bread

Now, if you're looking to get your feet wet learning to make real bread, this here's a good one for you. It's an all-purpose extra-basic yeast bread, and I used it on *The American Baking Competition.* It's easy to make and hard to screw up—but don't go trying, though! Y'all do have to use your brains a bit on this one, since yeast can be kind of temperamental. With the flour, you just have to feel out the quantities a bit and really pay attention to that dough. It might take more or less flour depending on your altitude or the humidity where you live. Like all good breads, this one rises twice, but you can leave it for a while on that first rise, go shopping or whatever, and come back to finish it off.

INGREDIENTS

4 teaspoons active dry yeast

½ cup warm water

½ cup plus 1 teaspoon sugar

2 cups whole milk, heated until warm to the touch

About 7½ cups all-purpose flour, plus more for kneading

7 tablespoons unsalted butter, melted, plus more for the bowl

2 large eggs

2 teaspoons salt

DIRECTIONS

Dissolve the yeast in the warm water with 1 teaspoon of the sugar; let stand until frothy.

Combine the yeast mixture, warm milk, remaining ½ cup sugar, and about 1 cup of the flour—enough to make a mixture the consistency of pancake batter—and beat thoroughly by hand or using a stand mixer with the paddle attachment. Add 3 tablespoons of the butter, the eggs, and salt and continue beating. Gradually add the remaining 6 to 6½ cups flour until a soft dough forms. Sprinkle a small amount of flour onto your counter and let the dough rest at room temperature for about 15 minutes.

Knead the dough until smooth and satiny; I use a stand mixer fitted with the dough hook and let it go for 4 to 5 minutes. Grease a bowl, add the dough, and turn it over in the bowl to grease all sides. Cover and let rise in a warm place until doubled in bulk, 1 to 1½ hours. Punch down and then turn out onto a floured board.

Preheat the oven to 350°F.

Punch down the dough and divide in half. Form into 2 cylinders and transfer to two 9 × 5-inch loaf pans. Let rise until doubled in size again, about 1 hour.

Bake until golden brown, 25 to 30 minutes. Remove from the oven and baste immediately with the remaining 4 tablespoons butter. Let cool in the pans on wire racks.

MAKES TWO 9 × 5-INCH LOAVES

 BLUE RIBBON TIP You can do a lot with this one—roll it out, braid it, make cinnamon bread, or even stuff it with something. When I'm basting it at the end, I like to use honey butter because I like that sweeter taste, but go ahead and play around with the recipe after trying it a few times. I'm a firm believer that one recipe can create five different dishes.

Mama's Corn Bread

In my house, hardly a day goes by without biscuits or corn bread, which I make every other day, it seems. This is Mama's recipe, and I'm sure it was Nana's and Great-Grandma's and Great-Great-Grandma's before. You have to use shortening or lard to preheat the pan, so that it gets really hot and the bread won't stick. Don't use butter or oil, because it'll burn. It's almost a requirement if you live around these parts to keep bacon drippings sitting in a jar somewhere; this is a good place to use them.

INGREDIENTS

- 1 tablespoon shortening (I use Crisco) or lard
- 2 cups self-rising cornmeal (I use White Lily)
- ¼ cup all-purpose flour
- 1 teaspoon salt
- 1 teaspoon baking soda
- 1¾ cups well-shaken buttermilk (see Blue Ribbon Tip, page 22)
- 2 large eggs
- 2 tablespoons bacon drippings, cooled (from about 4 strips of bacon)

DIRECTIONS

Preheat the oven to 450°F. Put the shortening in a 10-inch cast-iron skillet and put it in the oven as it heats.

Into a large bowl, sift together the cornmeal, flour, salt, and baking soda. Stir in the buttermilk, eggs, and drippings, mixing just until the dry ingredients are moistened and there are no clumps.

Carefully remove the skillet from the oven and pour in the batter. Bake until golden around the edges, 20 to 25 minutes. Serve warm.

MAKES ONE 10-INCH CORN BREAD

SODA BISCUITS (FOR Y'ALL WHO THINK YOU CAN'T MAKE BISCUITS)

If you think you can't make a biscuit, you can make these. They're like a traditional 7UP biscuit, but I use club soda instead so they're not so sweet. These are an important biscuit for me—I used them to catch me a husband! We'd been dating a bit and I invited Mark to supper. I made fried chicken, mashed potatoes, and home-style creamed corn. Now, I knew my buttermilk biscuits were not going to attract a man (since I hadn't made them right yet, even after forty-four years of trying!), so I made these. These and that blackberry cobbler (see page 149) for dessert got me a husband!

INGREDIENTS

2 cups Bisquick or Pioneer biscuit mix, plus more for kneading

½ cup sour cream

½ cup club soda

4 tablespoons (½ stick) unsalted butter, melted

DIRECTIONS

Preheat the oven to 450°F.

Put the biscuit mix in a large bowl and cut the sour cream into it, using a pastry cutter or fork. Stir in the club soda; the dough will be soft.

Turn the dough out onto a floured counter and knead 3 or 4 times, adding additional flour if needed. Press or pat the dough into a ½-inch-thick rectangle. Cut 9 biscuits.

Pour the butter into a 9-inch square baking pan. Arrange the biscuits in the pan on top of the melted butter.

Bake until golden brown, 12 to 15 minutes. Serve warm.

MAKES ABOUT 9 BISCUITS

BISCUITS LIKE NANA MADE

I'm about to admit something I never thought I would: I couldn't make a proper buttermilk biscuit until I turned forty-four. Nana tried to teach me all my life, but somehow I could never make them right—even when I watched her *and* used her recipe *and* practiced and practiced and practiced.

When I tried out for *The American Baking Competition,* we had to make something, but we didn't know what it would be. I saw all the ingredients out and all I could think was *Please, God, don't make me make biscuits!* I turned over that recipe page, and, of course, there it was: Southern-style biscuits. Within seconds there's a producer up in my face saying, "If there's anyone who can make Southern biscuits, it's you!" If only he knew. . . . But because I didn't have time to think or mess with them too long, they turned out perfect. And that's the special tip: The trick to making fluffy buttermilk biscuits is not to mess with them too much. If you overwork the dough, they'll get real tough—trust me, I spent most of my life doing that.

INGREDIENTS

- ½ cup (1 stick) unsalted butter or lard, cold, plus 2 tablespoons unsalted butter, cold, plus more for the pan

- 2¼ cups self-rising soft wheat flour (I use White Lily), plus more for kneading
- Pinch of salt

- 1¼ cups well-shaken buttermilk (see Blue Ribbon Tip, page 22)
- Chocolate Gravy (page 209), optional

 BLUE RIBBON TIPS I like lard because it makes the biscuits fluffier, but use butter if you prefer. I use the ring of a mason jar to cut these, so they turn out bigger (cat head–sized). If you're just using a basic biscuit cutter or smaller 2-inch round, you'll get more.

Make sure your biscuits touch when you cook them—it makes them bake up instead of out and they get all nice and poofy-like.

recipe continues

Preheat the oven to 425°F. Lightly grease a baking sheet.

Combine the flour and salt in a large bowl. Cut ½ cup of the butter into ¼-inch-thick slices and scatter on top of the flour. Using two forks or a pastry cutter, cut the butter into the flour until the butter is in small pieces. Add the buttermilk, stirring until just combined.

Turn the dough out onto a floured counter and knead 3 or 4 times, adding additional flour if needed. Press or pat the dough into a ½-inch-thick rectangle. Cut 8 to 12 biscuits (see Blue Ribbon Tips, page 205) and arrange, side by side and touching, on the baking sheet.

Bake until lightly browned, 15 to 20 minutes. Remove from the oven and rub the hot biscuits with the remaining 2 tablespoons butter to make the tops shiny. Serve warm, drizzled with chocolate gravy, if you like.

MAKES ABOUT 8 LARGE OR 12 SMALL BISCUITS

 BACON-CHEDDAR BISCUITS Cook 5 strips of bacon until crisp, chop them up, and add with 1 cup shredded Cheddar cheese to the dough.

Hoecakes

Hoecakes, which are like fried pancakes, are a tradition in the South, and this is an old family recipe. My great-grandmother had a story for everything. She told me that my great-great-uncle, who was a Confederate general, used to make and eat hoecakes during the Civil War. There wasn't a lot of meat, but the soldiers could always find some milk and eggs, so they would make these out in the field. Her stories always stuck with me and made me remember the recipe, too.

You have to have butter on hoecakes, but you can play around with whatever else you put on top. My kids eat these with syrup, but I like them with jam, jelly, or preserves. The cornmeal in these makes them a little less sweet than regular pancakes, which I like. You can make these with buttermilk or regular milk, but I personally like them with buttermilk.

INGREDIENTS

1½ cups self-rising cornmeal (I use White Lily)

⅔ cup well-shaken buttermilk (see Blue Ribbon Tip, page 22), or whole milk

1 large egg

½ teaspoon salt

About ⅔ cup vegetable oil, for frying

DIRECTIONS

In a large bowl, stir together the cornmeal, buttermilk, egg, and salt with a spoon.

Fill a large frying pan with a quarter inch of oil and heat until hot enough for frying; if you drop a pinch of flour into it, it should sizzle. Working in batches, drop the dough by heaping tablespoonful into the hot oil. Brown on one side, about 3 minutes, then turn and fry until puffy and golden brown on the second side, 3 minutes. Drain on paper towels. Serve hot.

MAKES ABOUT 15 HOECAKES

JONNYCaKES

Jonnycakes are exactly like Hoecakes (page 207), except hoecakes puff up and jonnycakes lie flat. Everybody in the South knows how to make them both—it's just something you're taught–and this recipe's been passed down in my family since the 1800s. We like to eat these real hot with butter and maple syrup or applesauce.

INGREDIENTS ....

1 cup white cornmeal
¾ teaspoon salt

½ cup whole milk

1½ tablespoons bacon drippings, plus more as needed

DIRECTIONS ....

In a medium bowl, combine the cornmeal and salt.

In a medium saucepan over high heat, bring 1 cup water to a rapid boil and then remove from the heat. Slowly dribble the boiling water into the cornmeal, stirring constantly. Stir in the milk; the mixture will be fairly thick.

Generously grease a large, heavy frying pan with the bacon drippings and set over medium heat. When the fat is hot, working in batches, drop the batter in by heaping tablespoonfuls. Flatten the batter with a spatula to a thickness of about ¼ inch. Fry until golden brown, about 3 minutes, then turn and brown on the other side, adding more bacon drippings as needed, 3 minutes. Drain on paper towels. Serve hot.

MaKES aBOUT 12 JONNYCaKES

CHOCOLATE GRAVY

I've been fed chocolate gravy all my life; we put it on anything that's kind of bland, like hoecakes, biscuits, or toast. Me, I'll just eat it out of the pot with a spoon, too! I put all the dry ingredients in a jar together and then cook some up when the kids are wanting it. It ain't good when it's cold, so don't even try it that way.

INGREDIENTS

1 cup sugar
1 tablespoon unsweetened cocoa powder

1 tablespoon self-rising flour (I use White Lily)
Pinch of salt

¼ teaspoon pure vanilla extract
1 tablespoon unsalted butter

DIRECTIONS

In a medium saucepan, combine the sugar, cocoa powder, flour, and salt. Stir in 1¼ cups water and the vanilla extract. Bring to a boil over medium heat and cook, stirring occasionally, until thick, about 15 minutes. Remove from the heat and add the butter. Serve warm.

MAKES ABOUT 1½ CUPS

BLUEBERRY MUFFINS AND A WAY OF LIFE

Everybody needs to eat blueberries. I found out through the lady who does my skin care that blueberries are just the best thing for your skin, and she's got a PhD in the stuff, so she knows what she's saying! If you eat blueberries every other day, your skin will be just perfect and beautiful, so get started on these muffins—it'll be a way of life. There's a blueberry farm right up here by the house, and it's nothing to go and pick blueberries in late spring. We come back with tons of them, so I make these easy muffins, which have a little applesauce in them for sweetness and texture.

INGREDIENTS

- 4 tablespoons (½ stick) unsalted butter, melted, plus more for the pans
- 1 cup sugar
- 2 cups all-purpose flour
- 1 tablespoon baking powder
- ½ teaspoon salt
- ½ cup unsweetened applesauce
- ½ cup whole milk
- ½ teaspoon pure vanilla extract
- 2 cups fresh or frozen blueberries

DIRECTIONS

Preheat the oven to 350°F. Line 12 muffin cups with paper liners or grease with butter.

In a bowl, in order, mix together the butter, sugar, flour, baking powder, salt, applesauce, milk, and vanilla extract. Fold in the blueberries. Divide the batter evenly among the muffin cups, filling each three-quarters full.

Bake until the tops are firm and a cake tester or toothpick inserted in the center of a muffin comes out clean, about 25 minutes. Let cool for 10 minutes in the pans, before turning out onto wire racks to cool at least slightly.

MAKES 12 MUFFINS

CHEESE MUFFINS

I think I might have gotten this recipe, or at least the idea for it, from a Julia Child demo I went to when I was just nine or ten years old. The whole Girl Scout troop went, and I was just in heaven. Julia Child was my Miley Cyrus and my Justin Bieber all at once. I love, love, love cheese and I like to make these for a brunch- or breakfast-type thing; they're real good with scrambled eggs, bacon, and hash browns.

INGREDIENTS

- 1 cup (2 sticks) unsalted butter, melted, plus more for the pans
- 1¼ cups whole milk
- 2 large eggs
- 3½ cups all-purpose flour
- 2 teaspoons baking powder
- ½ teaspoon salt
- 1½ cups cubed Cheddar cheese

DIRECTIONS

Preheat the oven to 350°F. Grease 12 muffin cups.

In a large bowl, whisk together the milk, eggs, and butter. Add the flour, baking powder, salt, and cheese and mix, stirring with a wooden spoon, until just combined. Do not overmix. Spoon the mixture evenly into the muffin cups.

Bake until golden brown on top and a cake tester or toothpick inserted in the center of a muffin comes out clean, 15 to 20 minutes. Let cool for 10 minutes in the pans, before turning out onto wire racks to cool at least slightly.

MAKES 12 MUFFINS

CHOCOLATE CHIP CRUMBLE MUFFINS

The kids are always asking for these muffins. I used to make them as plain chocolate muffins, but when I learned to make streusel topping, I started doing them this way, and now I can't go back. I'm one of those people who only eats the top of that muffin—I will not eat the rest—so I like to make them extra-large so that muffin top's extra-large, too!

INGREDIENTS

topping
- ⅓ cup all-purpose flour
- ¼ cup firmly packed light brown sugar
- ¼ teaspoon ground cinnamon
- 3 tablespoons unsalted butter, cut into pieces, at room temperature
- ⅓ cup mini chocolate chips

muffins
- 1½ cups all-purpose flour
- ½ cup unsweetened cocoa powder
- 1 teaspoon baking powder
- 1 teaspoon baking soda
- ½ teaspoon salt
- ½ cup (1 stick) unsalted butter, at room temperature
- 1 cup granulated sugar
- 3 large eggs
- 1 teaspoon pure vanilla extract
- 1¼ cups sour cream

DIRECTIONS

Preheat the oven to 375°F. Line 24 regular-sized muffin cups with paper liners, or 12 extra-large muffin cups with paper liners.

Make the topping: Using an electric mixer, beat the flour, brown sugar, and cinnamon on low speed. Add the butter and mix until large crumbs form. Add the chocolate chips and stir just until they are evenly dispersed throughout the crumbs.

Make the muffins: Sift together the flour, cocoa powder, baking powder, baking soda, and salt.

Using an electric mixer, beat the butter on medium speed until it is light and fluffy. Mix in the granulated sugar. Add the eggs, one at a time, and then mix in the vanilla extract. Alternate adding the flour mixture and the sour cream, starting and ending with the flour, and mixing until just combined.

Scoop the batter into the muffin cups, filling them about halfway. Spoon the topping onto the top of the batter. Bake until the topping is golden brown and a cake tester or toothpick inserted in the center of a muffin comes out clean, 20 to 25 minutes for regular-sized muffins, 25 to 30 minutes for extra large. Let cool for 10 minutes in the pans, before turning out onto wire racks to cool at least slightly.

MAKES 24 REGULAR OR
12 EXTRA-LARGE MUFFINS

DONUT MUFFINS

These taste just like donuts, but with a quarter of the work. I found this recipe in one of Mama's books; it was from a women's-gathering thing at the church, I think. I saw something that said "donut muffins" when I was looking through it, and I knew I had to make them. Lord knows, I love donuts! These are kind of puffy on the inside, like donuts should be, and puffier than you would think a muffin could be.

INGREDIENTS ....

muffins

4 tablespoons (½ stick) unsalted butter, at room temperature, plus more for the pans

¼ cup vegetable oil

½ cup granulated sugar

⅓ cup firmly packed light brown sugar

2 large eggs

1½ teaspoons baking powder

¼ teaspoon baking soda

¾ teaspoon ground allspice

1 teaspoon ground cinnamon

¾ teaspoon salt

1 teaspoon pure vanilla extract

2⅔ cups all-purpose flour

1 cup whole milk

glaze

1 cup confectioner's sugar, sifted

3 tablespoons unsalted butter, melted

2 tablespoons hot water

¾ teaspoon pure vanilla extract

DIRECTIONS ....

Preheat the oven to 425°F. Grease 12 muffin cups or line with paper liners.

Make the muffins: Using an electric mixer, beat together the butter, vegetable oil, and both sugars until smooth. Beat in the eggs, one at a time. With the mixer on low speed, beat in the baking powder, baking soda, allspice, cinnamon, salt, and vanilla until just combined. Alternate adding the flour and milk, starting and ending with the flour, and mixing until just combined. Do not overmix! Spoon the batter equally into the muffin cups. Bake until the muffin tops are pale golden and springy to the touch and a cake tester or toothpick inserted in the center of a muffin comes out clean, 15 to 17 minutes. Let the muffins cool in the pans for 5 minutes, then unmold onto wire racks and let cool for 10 minutes before glazing.

Make the glaze: In a medium bowl, whisk together the confectioner's sugar, butter, hot water, and vanilla extract until smooth.

Dip the top of each muffin into the glaze, set upright, and allow the glaze to harden. Once hardened, dip a second time and allow to harden again before serving.

MAKES 12 MUFFINS

LEMON STREUSEL MUFFINS

Nana used to make these for me because I love lemon. She told me that this recipe was actually brought over from Ireland, passed down from her grandmother to her mother to her. I'm sure it's changed some over the years, but these are a real good solid lemon muffin with a little extra sweetness from that white chocolate. I've made them for baby showers and a lot of breakfasts and brunches.

INGREDIENTS

topping

- ½ cup all-purpose flour
- 3 tablespoons granulated sugar
- 1 tablespoon light brown sugar
- ⅛ teaspoon salt
- 3 tablespoons unsalted butter, melted
- 1 teaspoon pure vanilla extract

muffins

- 1 cup well-shaken buttermilk (see Blue Ribbon Tip, page 22)
- 1 cup old-fashioned rolled oats
- ½ cup white chocolate chips
- ½ cup (1 stick) unsalted butter, melted, plus more for the pan
- 1½ cups self-rising flour (I use White Lily)
- ¼ teaspoon salt
- 1 tablespoon grated lemon zest (from about 2 lemons)
- ½ cup firmly packed light brown sugar
- 1 large egg, beaten
- ½ teaspoon lemon extract

DIRECTIONS

Make the topping: In a small bowl, stir together the all-purpose flour, both sugars, and the salt. Use a fork or your fingers to mix in the butter and vanilla until thoroughly incorporated. Cover and chill in the refrigerator until ready to use.

Make the muffins: Combine the buttermilk, oats, and white chocolate chips. Cover and let sit at room temperature for 30 minutes so the oats soak up the milk.

Preheat the oven to 375°F. Grease 12 muffin cups or line with paper liners.

In a medium bowl, whisk together the self-rising flour and salt.

Stir the lemon zest and brown sugar into the oat mixture and then whisk in the egg, butter, and lemon extract. Using a wooden spoon, stir in the flour mixture until just incorporated.

Scoop the batter evenly into the muffin cups. The cups will be full; these muffins don't rise much. Remove the topping from the refrigerator and break the pieces into small clumps. Top each muffin cup with about 1 heaping tablespoon of streusel topping.

Bake the muffins until a cake tester or toothpick inserted in the center of a muffin comes out with only a few crumbs attached, 15 to 20 minutes. Let cool for 10 minutes in the pan before turning out onto wire racks to cool at least slightly.

MAKES 12 MUFFINS

 BLUE RIBBON TIP Melt some white chocolate chips to drizzle over the topping for that fancy bakery look. But be careful with white chocolate; it has a high butterfat content and you don't want to burn it. Melt it in a double boiler over simmering water and stir it often; this will make it smooth, not chunky, and help prevent it from burning.

CANDY & TRUFFLES

chapter
8

aunt THeLma's peanut butter BaLLs

This here recipe's top secret—up until now, no one knew it but me! I have never given it out, but these are just so doggone good, I couldn't write a chapter about candies and not include these peanut butter balls. My aunt Thelma came up with this recipe, taught it to me when I was eight or nine, and made me promise that I wouldn't tell anyone in the family how to make them. When she passed on when I was thirteen, I had to start doing them for everybody. Last year I probably made 1,500 of them! The nuts, peanut butter, and graham cracker crumbs give them a great hearty texture.

INGREDIENTS ....

- 2 cups creamy peanut butter (I use Jif)
- ½ cup plus 2 tablespoons (1¼ sticks) unsalted butter, at room temperature
- 2 teaspoons pure vanilla extract
- ⅛ teaspoon salt
- 2 cups confectioner's sugar
- 2 cups chopped pecans
- 2 to 2½ cups graham cracker crumbs (28 to 35 crackers; see Blue Ribbon Tip, below)
- 2 cups semisweet chocolate chips

 BLUE RIBBON TIP If you end up using one of those natural peanut butters that have a lot of extra oil, use that extra ½ cup of graham cracker crumbs; if not, you're probably fine with just those 2 cups. And while I usually suggest heating your chocolate in a microwave, on account of how easy it is, with this recipe it's best to use a double boiler so you don't have to keep reheating that chocolate, as it may harden a bit.

Using an electric mixer, beat together the peanut butter, ½ cup of the butter, the vanilla, and salt. Stir in the confectioner's sugar, pecans, and 2 cups of the cracker crumbs.

Using your hands, roll the mixture into 1-inch balls. Set the balls in a single layer on a small wax paper–lined baking sheet and refrigerate until firm.

Melt the chocolate chips and remaining 2 tablespoons butter in the top half of a double boiler over simmering water, stirring until the chocolate has melted. Turn off the heat, but leave the chocolate over the hot water to prevent the chocolate from hardening. Insert a toothpick into a chilled peanut butter ball and dip into the melted chocolate until coated. Return the ball to the baking sheet, removing the toothpick. Repeat with the remaining balls and then chill in the refrigerator until hardened. Store in an airtight container in the refrigerator.

MAKES ABOUT 40 BALLS

southern pralines

Everybody needs to eat pralines at least once, because they are like potato chips: After just one, you'll be hooked. I found this recipe in an old cookbook of my Daddy's. I've always loved pralines, especially because pecans are my favorite, and I started making them out of that book when I was fifteen years old. I used to live in New Orleans, where they first came up with them, so I always think of that city when I make these. Around Christmastime I'll make up a bunch and put them in my Christmas baskets with all my other goodies.

INGREDIENTS

2 cups firmly packed
light brown sugar

¼ cup evaporated milk

2 cups pecan pieces

2 teaspoons pure
vanilla extract

3 tablespoons
unsalted butter,
cut into pieces, cold

DIRECTIONS

Line a baking sheet with wax paper.
Combine the brown sugar, evaporated milk, and ¼ cup water in a medium saucepan and bring to a boil, stirring constantly, over medium heat. Cook until the mixture reaches 235°F on a candy thermometer or the soft-ball stage (see Blue Ribbon Tip, page 193).

Remove from the heat and stir in the pecans, vanilla, and butter. Immediately drop by tablespoons onto the baking sheet. Leave at room temperature; the pralines will spread out and harden. Store in an airtight container, separating the layers with wax paper.

makes about 20 pralines

salted caramels

I know salted caramel's all the rage now, but this recipe was passed around by Nana's church group years ago. She used to make them at Christmastime and sprinkle them with kosher salt at the end. We would hide the caramels around her house so that we were the only ones that got to eat them. These are a real nice homemade gift for the holidays, especially in some pretty colored wrappers.

INGREDIENTS

Nonstick cooking spray

1 cup heavy cream

5 tablespoons unsalted butter, cubed

1 teaspoon coarse sea salt, plus more for topping

1½ cups sugar

¼ cup light corn syrup

1½ teaspoons pure vanilla extract

DIRECTIONS

Line an 8-inch square baking pan with parchment paper, leaving overhang on two opposite sides, and spray lightly with nonstick spray; set aside.

In a small saucepan, bring the heavy cream, butter, and salt to a boil. Remove from the heat and keep warm.

In a large saucepan over high heat, stir together the sugar, corn syrup, and ¼ cup water until the sugar is dissolved. Boil without stirring (you can gently swirl the entire saucepan occasionally to ensure even heating) until the mixture turns a light golden caramel color. Lower the heat so that the caramel simmers and then very carefully pour the cream mixture into the saucepan. Stirring constantly, cook the mixture until it reaches a temperature of 250°F on a candy thermometer or the hard-ball stage (see Blue Ribbon Tip, page 193) and is thick and amber in color. Remove from the heat and carefully stir in the vanilla extract.

Pour the mixture into the baking pan and let sit for 30 minutes. Sprinkle with a little sea salt and then let cool completely at room temperature, about 1 hour 30 minutes more.

Remove the caramel from the baking pan by lifting the parchment paper. Using a very sharp, warm knife, cut the caramel into 1-inch squares. Wrap in candy wrappers or store in an airtight container.

makes 40 caramels

redNeck FreNcH TruFFLeS

I was one of the lucky ones who got to try Biscoff spread before they had it here in the States—a friend of mine who lives overseas sent it to me because she knew I would like it. It's like Nutella made with crushed butter cookies instead of chocolate and hazelnuts. And, just like Nutella, it's good straight off a spoon, but it also makes a good truffle, creamy and sweet. I use vanilla wafers to break up the sweetness of the Biscoff and chocolate. These are a little something different on the candy tray for the holidays. I call them "redneck" because I came up with them!

INGREDIENTS

½ cup semisweet
chocolate chips

½ cup Biscoff spread

1½ cups crushed vanilla
wafers

6 ounces white
almond bark

DIRECTIONS

Melt the chocolate chips in a microwave or double boiler. Remove from the heat and stir in the Biscoff spread and then the vanilla wafers. Using your hands, roll into tablespoon-and-a-half-sized balls and put on a wax paper–lined baking sheet. Let sit at room temperature for 20 minutes.

Melt the bark in the top half of a double boiler over simmering water, stirring until the chocolate has melted. Turn off the heat, but leave the chocolate over the hot water to prevent the chocolate from hardening. Insert a toothpick into a ball and dip into the melted chocolate until coated. Return the ball to the baking sheet, removing the toothpick. Repeat with the remaining balls. Set aside until the chocolate sets. Store in an airtight container, separating the layers with wax paper.

MAKES 18 TO 20 TruFFLeS

oreo Truffles

My friend Deanna lives in Florida and makes the absolute best cake balls in the whole free world; she's an amazing baker and friend. One day we were on the phone, talking about baking, of course, when I said, "Why don't we do truffles with crushed-up Oreos and cream cheese?" She tried it and it worked and we came up with this recipe, which I just love to make all the time—there are only three ingredients in it.

I love Oreos, but I think they should be seasonal. I know they got the mint ones for winter and the orange ones around Halloween, but I think the regular cookies are just too readily available—I can't stop buying (and eating) them!

INGREDIENTS ....

1 (18-ounce) package
Oreo cookies, finely
crushed

1 (8-ounce) package
cream cheese, at
room temperature

1 (15-ounce) package
almond bark

DIRECTIONS ....

Using a spoon, mix the crushed cookies and cream cheese until fully combined. Using your hands, form tablespoon-sized balls and then freeze on a baking sheet until firm, about 15 minutes.

Melt the bark in the top half of a double boiler over simmering water, stirring until the chocolate has melted. Turn off the heat, but leave the chocolate over the hot water to prevent the chocolate from hardening. Insert a toothpick into a chilled ball and dip into the melted chocolate until coated. Return the ball to the baking sheet, removing the toothpick. Repeat with the remaining balls. Set aside until the chocolate sets. Store in an airtight container, separating the layers with wax paper.

MAKES 26 TO 30 TRUFFLES

cake BaLLS for THe FaInT of HearT

People are scared to make cake balls because they're scared of screwing them up. You heard it here first: You can't screw cake balls up! Deanna, the queen of cake balls (honest to God, she can make cake balls out of anything you can buy on the shelf), and I came up with this on the phone. She's one of the best baking friends I ever had and we just love making things up together, even though she lives all the way in Florida. You can use any kind of cake mix that you want; I've made them out of carrot, vanilla, and chocolate cake mixes, but red velvet is my favorite—which is weird, because I don't usually like red velvet cake.

INGREDIENTS

1 (12-ounce) box red velvet cake mix
Eggs, oil, and water, as directed on the box

1 (16-ounce) can cream cheese frosting

1 (24-ounce) package chocolate almond bark (regular or white chocolate flavor)

DIRECTIONS

Bake the cake in a 9 × 13-inch baking pan according to the package directions. After the cake has cooled completely, crumble into a large bowl. Mix in the cream cheese frosting and then roll the mixture into quarter-sized balls. Lay on wax paper–lined baking sheets and chill until firm, 2 to 4 hours in the refrigerator, or 1 to 2 hours in the freezer.

Melt the bark in the top half of a double boiler over simmering water, stirring until the chocolate has melted. Turn off the heat, but leave the chocolate over the hot water to prevent the chocolate from hardening. Insert a toothpick into a chilled ball and dip into the melted chocolate until coated. Return the ball to the baking sheet, removing the toothpick. Repeat with the remaining balls. Set aside until the chocolate sets. Store in an airtight container, separating the layers with wax paper.

MaKeS 45 TO 50 Cake BaLLS

Nana's Christmas Fudge

I can tell you two things about this recipe: Number one, Nana made the best fudge in the world, and number two, Nana made the best fudge in the world. This fudge is so old-school that the recipe wasn't even written down—just another thing I had to remember over the years. But that's how my memory works, I guess. I can't tell you what I wore the first day of school, but I can tell you what I made when I was four years old. I spent many a day standing on a chair at the counter stirring and stirring this with Nana at Christmastime.

INGREDIENTS

- 4 tablespoons (½ stick) unsalted butter, plus more for the pans
- 2 cups sugar
- ½ cup unsweetened cocoa powder
- 1 cup whole milk
- 1 teaspoon pure vanilla extract

DIRECTIONS

Grease an 8-inch square baking pan. Butter the sides of a medium saucepan to keep the sugar from sticking. In the saucepan, combine the sugar, cocoa powder, and milk over medium heat and bring to a boil, stirring constantly. Reduce the heat so the mixture simmers. Do not stir again. Cook until the temperature reaches 238°F on a candy thermometer or the soft-ball stage (see Blue Ribbon Tip, page 193).

Remove from the heat and add the butter and vanilla extract. Beat with a wooden spoon until the fudge loses its sheen, about 10 minutes. Do not underbeat. Pour into the prepared pan and refrigerate until cool. Cut into small squares and then store in an airtight container.

Makes about 25 pieces

LIQUORED-UP FUDGE

I also like to call this recipe "How to Have a Happy Family Christmas."
This is an adult-friendly treat. Don't let the kids near it—it's real strong! Since you don't cook it, the booze doesn't burn off. We always joke that after you eat this, if a cop stops you, just say, "No, sir, I haven't been drinking, just eating fudge."

INGREDIENTS

Unsalted butter, for the pan

1 (12-ounce) bag semisweet chocolate chips

2 (1-pound) boxes confectioner's sugar

1 cup Jack Daniel's whiskey

2 teaspoons pure vanilla extract

1 teaspoon pure almond extract

1 cup chopped pecans (optional)

DIRECTIONS

Butter a 9 × 13-inch baking pan, line with parchment paper, and butter the paper as well.

Melt the chocolate chips in a microwave or double boiler, stirring frequently.

Mix together the confectioner's sugar, whiskey, and extracts in a large bowl. Stir in the melted chocolate and the nuts, if using. Pour into the prepared pan and cover with plastic wrap. Let cool until set, but still warm enough to cut easily into squares. Store in an airtight container.

MAKES ABOUT 30 PIECES

easy peanut butter fudge

I'm a firm believer in "the easier, the better." This is a no-fail recipe with just four ingredients. I make this for my husband, Mark, the peanut butter guy. He's my number-one cheerleader and supporter, and that's why this tasty fudge is in the book! Assemble and measure all your ingredients before you begin, as you will be stirring constantly once you start.

INGREDIENTS

Unsalted butter, for the pan

2 cups sugar

½ cup whole milk

1 teaspoon pure vanilla extract

¾ cup creamy peanut butter (I use Jif)

DIRECTIONS

Butter an 8-inch square baking dish.

In a medium saucepan over medium heat, bring the sugar and milk to a boil, stirring constantly. Once bubbles form throughout the entire mixture, continue boiling for exactly 2½ minutes.

Remove from the heat and stir in the vanilla extract and then the peanut butter. Blend well with a wooden spoon, stirring quickly until smooth. Pour into the buttered dish and smooth the top. Let cool completely before cutting into pieces. Store in an airtight container.

MAKES ABOUT 25 PIECES

OLD ENGLISH TOFFEE

How'd I get this recipe? From my ex-stepmother-in-law—would you believe it? They live in Indianapolis, and she'd make this in the wintertime. I can't tell you how many pieces it makes, because she'd cook it up, put it in the garage, and it would instantly freeze. Then we'd break it up into big and small pieces with our hands and just get to eating it right then!

INGREDIENTS

- 1 cup (2 sticks) unsalted butter, plus more for the pan
- 1 cup sugar
- 1 tablespoon light corn syrup
- 6 ounces semisweet chocolate chips
- ¼ cup finely chopped almonds

DIRECTIONS

Line a large jelly-roll pan with aluminum foil. Grease the foil thoroughly.

Melt the butter in a medium saucepan over medium heat. Add the sugar and bring to a boil, stirring constantly. Stir in 2 tablespoons water and the corn syrup. Cook, stirring constantly, until the mixture thickens, turns a light brown toffee color, and reaches 250°F on a candy thermometer or the hard-ball stage (see Blue Ribbon Tip, page 193).

Remove from the heat and pour onto the baking pan. Carefully spread the toffee, using a heatproof spatula, until it is about ¼ inch thick. Immediately sprinkle the chocolate chips on top and use the spatula to gently coat the entire layer of toffee with the melting chocolate. Sprinkle the chopped nuts on top and then let cool completely.

When firm, break into pieces. Store in an airtight container.

MAKES ABOUT 2½ POUNDS TOFFEE

Peppermint Truffles

I do these at Christmastime. It's another candy that goes in those baskets that everyone waits on all year long. Since I have to make so many around the holidays, I refuse to make them any other time of year. They're real minty and classic, perfect for eating under the Christmas tree with a big cup of hot chocolate.

INGREDIENTS

- 4 regular peppermint candy canes
- 6 ounces semisweet chocolate, finely chopped
- ½ cup heavy cream
- ½ teaspoon peppermint extract
- 2 tablespoons unsalted butter, at room temperature
- 1 pound chocolate almond bark

DIRECTIONS

Pulse the candy canes in a food processor until crushed into small pieces.

Put the chocolate in a heatproof bowl. Heat the cream in a small saucepan until it is almost boiling and bubbles appear around the edges. Pour the cream over the chocolate and let sit for 1 minute. Whisk until the chocolate is smooth and melted. Add the mint extract and butter and whisk until the butter melts and your ganache is silky smooth. Stir in most of the crushed candy canes, reserving a few tablespoons to use as garnish. Press plastic wrap onto the top of the ganache and refrigerate until it is firm enough to scoop, about 2 hours. If you leave it too long, it may be hard to work with; let it soften at room temperature if that happens.

Scoop 1½ teaspoons of the ganache and then roll between your palms to make balls. Put the truffles on wax paper–lined baking sheets and return to the refrigerator.

Melt the bark in the top half of a double boiler over simmering water, stirring until the chocolate has melted. Turn off the heat, but leave the chocolate over the hot water to prevent the chocolate from hardening. Insert a toothpick into a chilled ball and dip into the melted chocolate until coated. Return the ball to the baking sheet, removing the toothpick. Repeat with the remaining balls. While the chocolate is still wet, sprinkle the tops with the reserved crushed candy canes. Set aside until the chocolate sets. Store in an airtight container.

MAKES 40 TRUFFLES

acknowledgments

There are so many people I would like to thank . . .

Sarablake, my daughter, for making me a mama and keeping me on my toes.

Mark, my husband and CEO (chief eating officer), for standing by me so I can live my dreams and for pushing me to not be scared to jump.

Effie, my friend, my rock, thank you for your support. I love you.

Carlo, words can't describe how much you mean to me. I love you, friend.

Sharon Bowers, for taking a chance on a country girl, the best agent a girl could have.

Leah Baba, without your mad grammar skills I couldn't have done this; thank you.

Rica Allannic, for being the world's best editor and believing in this book as much as I do.

Ben Fink, your ability to capture the passion in my food is amazing; you're the best.

Erin McDowell, you're a rockin' food stylist; bourbon love, my girl.

Barb Fritz, for finding just the right plates for the photos.

Ashley Tucker, thank you for making the design of my book something I can't stop looking at.

Pam Krauss, Doris Cooper, Amy Boorstein, Heather Williamson, Stephanie Huntwork, Jane Treuhaft, Jim Massey, Erica Gelbard, Carly Gorga, and all the folks at Clarkson Potter who made this book come to life!

To all my fans, without y'all I couldn't do what I love—and that's share the baking love.

And finally, a very special thank you to Jeff Foxworthy, for believing in me and being a part of my dream come true.

INDEX